T0335202

GOD AT WORK IN THE WORLD

THE WORLD

Theology and Mission in the Global Church

LALSANGKIMA PACHUAU

Baker Academic
a division of Baker Publishing Group
Grand Rapids, Michigan

Published by Baker Academic
a division of Baker Publishing Group
PO Box 6287, Grand Rapids, MI 49516-6287
www.bakeracademic.com

Printed in the United States of America

Library of Congress Cataloging-in-Publication Data
Names: Pachuau, Lalsangkima, author.
Title: God at work in the world : theology and mission in the global church / Lalsangkima Pachuau.
Description: Grand Rapids, MI : Baker Academic, a division of Baker Publishing Group, [2022] | Includes index.
Identifiers: LCCN 2021046038 | ISBN 9781540961365 (paperback) | ISBN 9781540965660 (casebound) | ISBN 9781493436866 (pdf) | ISBN 9781493436859 (ebook)
Subjects: LCSH: Missions. | Salvation—Christianity.
Classification: LCC BV2061.3 .P335 2022 | DDC 266—dc23
LC record available at https://lccn.loc.gov/2021046038

Baker Publishing Group publications use paper produced from sustainable forestry practices and post-consumer waste whenever possible.

22   23   24   25   26   27   28   7   6   5   4   3   2   1

"One complaint from the colonial era concerned Western theology's implicit claims of the universality of its local embodiments of the Christian faith. Our constructive response lies in discovering the nature of the gospel's universality within its different embodiments across times and cultures and in discussion with a multitude of contexts. This is Kima's intent: to open the formal theological enterprise to the challenges in method and material as they exist within world Christianity. While one might like to push Kima further in the direction he has initiated, the first step on a such an unsettling journey is always the most difficult. *God at Work in the World* is a beacon on that path, and it must be congratulated."

—**John G. Flett**, Pilgrim Theological College, The University of Divinity, Melbourne, Australia

"Pachuau offers us a refreshing and reinvigorating theology of our working God, with whom we are called to work in the tasks of renewal, reconciliation, and the rejuvenation of our relationship with God and with one another in the places where we live, study, work, face shared challenges, and worship within an interfaith and ecumenical reality. This book reminds us of the possibilities of sharing, caring, interacting, and witnessing to God's ongoing love for the world and all people—a task informed by renewed biblical exegesis, the rereading of debates and discussions in the early church, and the reclamation of a theological heritage that testifies to how we can work with our working God in embracing and transforming our world."

—**J. Jayakiran Sebastian**, United Lutheran Seminary

"In this notable book, Pachuau explores the vital frontier between a theology of mission rooted in the *missio Dei* and the more often neglected connections with Christology and ecclesiology that are so essential for a biblical and robust understanding of the mission of God. In a day when the *missio Dei* is frequently and awkwardly disconnected from the life and witness of the church, Pachuau restores that vital connection in many reflective and surprising ways. This book is also a rich conversation between disciplines that listens to voices from around the world and back through time. This is Pachuau at his best. May *God at Work in the World* be widely read!"

—**Timothy C. Tennent**, Asbury Theological Seminary

"Although there are many books about mission theology, few engage the work of theologians as deeply as this one does. Moreover, Pachuau widens the field to include global as well as Western works.

The splendid result challenges any mission activity that is not rooted in reflection on the mission of the triune God and on the contextual nature of all theologies."

—**Kirsteen Kim**, Fuller Theological Seminary

"*God at Work in the World* is the work of a mature scholar who has pondered the questions of mission, salvation, Christology, ecclesiology, and global culture over a lifetime of scholarship and teaching. It is a work that is the product of wide reading, not only of major Western scholars but also of scholars from the majority world—as a book on global Christianity should be. Pachuau has offered to fellow scholars and students around the world a firm introduction to the theology of mission that is not only profound but also accessible and sometimes even provocative. His approach is balanced, thoughtful, and ecumenically sensitive and will be an important addition to any theological or missiological library."

—**Stephen Bevans**, Catholic Theological Union, Chicago (emeritus)

"The intimate connection between Christian mission and theology has been receiving fresh attention with a growing awareness that the two are inextricably bound together. In this volume, Pachuau makes an important contribution to this developing conversation and its ongoing significance for the church in its local and global expressions. Anyone interested in the relationship between theology and mission will benefit from the clear and concise wisdom offered in this valuable work."

—**John R. Franke**, Second Presbyterian Church, Indianapolis;
author of *Missional Theology*

"*God at Work in the World* delves into some of the most pertinent and persistent theological themes at the heart of modern missiology with rare probity and passion. Comprehensive in its scope and compelling in its style, this work pries open the myriad ways in which theology informs and transforms mission, inviting readers to revisit this intersection from a global perspective. All in all, this is a timely and telling reminder that the only way for mission to be or become the heartbeat of the church in a changing world is to stay in rhythm with the will and work of God in our world today."

—**Peniel Rajkumar**, United Society Partners in the Gospel;
Ripon College Cuddesdon, Oxford

To

my sisters,
Ms. Lalthanpuii
Ms. Lalruatthangi (Mami)

my brothers,
Mr. Lalsawmliana Pachuau
Upa Lalrochuanga Pachuau (Mama)

and my very special niece,
Ms. Margaret Lalhruaitluangi (Matei)

Ever grateful to be in your company

CONTENTS

EXPANDED TABLE OF CONTENTS

PREFACE

To teach is to be taught. A true teacher—if there is one—must be a genuine student. After teaching more than two decades, mostly in India and the United States, I realize how much I have learned from my students. Quite common among the courses I have offered are those that have "theology of mission" in them either explicitly or as an implicit driving force. The chapters in this book germinated, grew, and matured in these classes. I owe a depth of gratitude to my students in these classes at the United Theological College (Bangalore, India) and at Asbury Theological Seminary (Wilmore, Kentucky). The materials in their present form will be most familiar to the PhD students in my Biblical Theology of Mission class and the master's students in the Bible and Theology of Mission class at Asbury Seminary.

The planning and writing of this book began slowly during school breaks. Without the generous sabbatical program of Asbury Theological Seminary, the book would not have been completed. Not only did the seminary grant me a six-month sabbatical leave; it also provided me funds for travel. Some of the chapters were presented as lectures at Bishop's College (Kolkata, India), Singapore Bible College, and Trinity Theological College (Singapore). The invaluable thoughts and ideas I gained in these interactions contributed to the revision of these chapters. I thank my good friend Dr. Sunil Caleb, the principal of Bishop's College, for the honor of delivering a lecture at my alma mater's bicentennial. In Singapore, a team of friends and

xiv   Preface

colleagues—including Dr. Samuel Law (senior dean of academic affairs, Singapore Bible College), Dr. Kwa Kiem Kiok (Biblical Graduate School of Theology), and Dr. Andrew Peh (Trinity Theological College)—arranged a series of lectures and seminars where I presented some of the chapters of this book together with other topics. The warm and scholarly responses I received from the lectures at Bishop's College, Singapore Bible College, and Trinity Theological College reshaped some of my ideas and built my confidence to push forward the thoughts presented in this book.

The encouragement and support of colleagues and friends have been essential to this work. There are far too many names to be mentioned. I absolutely enjoyed working with Mr. Jim Kinney, executive vice president of Baker Academic, and his team of skilled editors. Jim has been with me from the planning to the fruition of this book, and I owe him a great deal. Behind his unobtrusive and gentle manner is a great editing skill that made the writing of this book much easier.

INTRODUCTION

A Theological Viewpoint on Christian Missions

In treading the worlds of academia and Christian faith through theological studies, I often find myself not knowing where to step next. At one academic conference, I met an expert in Buddhism teaching in a well-known university who responded to my introduction as a teacher of Christian missions by telling me that he did not like Christian missions. He said something to the effect that Christian missions are imperialistic and missionaries are colonialists. My first inclination was to say that not all Christian missionaries are colonialists and to ask what he thought about Buddhist missions. Instead I proceeded cordially, turning the conversation into a theological exchange. I told him that my understanding of missions has to do with God's mission[1] out of his love for the world, which I believe was best expressed in Jesus's self-sacrifice. Therefore, true missions witnesses to such sacrificial love. The Buddhist scholar did not object to such an idea, and we happily discussed the power of sacrificial love. It appears to me that for this person, missions as a Christian practice has nothing

---

1. In this work, the word "mission" (singular) refers to God's redemptive work or mission on behalf of his creation. "Missions" (plural) refers to the varied works and activities of the church to reflect and participate in God's mission. For a good discussion, see Timothy Tennent, *Invitation to World Missions: Trinitarian Missiology for the Twenty-First Century* (Grand Rapids: Kregel, 2010), 54–59.

to do with God's act of love. It only denotes an invasion of innocent people groups by Christians who want to convert them to their kind of Christian religion.

On another occasion, my wife and I visited a church that we came to like very much. We especially loved the pastor's sermons and the congregation's genuine friendliness. As we became more involved in the church, I heard a story that puzzled me. It was the story of how the church's missions committee came to support a missions agency working among women in Latin America and Africa. An important factor in the committee's decision was whether the organization not be interested in conversion. Surprised, I inquired further, and one of the members said that she "would not want to support any kind of conversion." If I were to have identified a dominant theme in the sermons of the pastor, it would have been "transformation," which to me is another term for conversion. The pastor often called for change toward Christlikeness, but it was obvious that some in the congregation did not connect this with the concept of conversion.

These two stories illustrate the need for a theological understanding of mission. In both cases, my conversation partners had no problem with the underlying theology of the missionary's work, but a narrow perception of "missions" led them to resist it. While some objections to missions are simplistic and unfounded, some of the practices of missions are also unjust and even un-Christian, at least from a theological viewpoint. The disconnect between theology and practice can rob the missionary enterprise of its greatest asset—namely, a firm and credible biblical foundation—and the missionary's disregard of theology has often made Christian missions a questionable undertaking. While it may serve as a corrective to the practice or as a justification of the enterprise, theology of mission is more than these. Because Christianity by nature is missionary—as will be argued in a later chapter—any theological reflections on the Christian faith must have a missional component.

Theology of mission is an essential part of theology itself, and any theology that does not deal with God's mission cannot be fully regarded as theology proper. Theology of mission is not an appendix to the discipline of theology; instead, its locale is theology in its most basic sense of the term. In the second half of the twentieth century, the idea of mission was reconceptualized such that God's redemptive mission was understood as the foundation of the Christian missionary enterprise. Because of this shift in understanding, theologians now recognize the essentiality of the theology of mission for the entire enterprise of theology. The oft-quoted words of Martin Kähler that "mission is 'the mother of theology'"[2] seem increasingly agreeable to theologians. In locating theology of mission at the core of theology proper, I do not propose a different direction for theology or a revision of its meaning. My wish is to go back to the most fundamental meaning of theology and identify its missionary dimension.

My goal is to make good connections between Christian practice and its underlying beliefs. By articulating why we do what we do, we can both clarify the foundations of our actions and identify practices to purge. The realization that much of what was called "Christian missions" ended up being seen only as colonialism seems to have resulted in three different attitudes: (1) holding aggressively to the practices to preserve a hallowed tradition, (2) abandoning the enterprise or toning it down to an ineffective level, or (3) resolving to do it better. Many progressive "liberal" Christians uncritically conflate Christian missions and colonialism and abandon the enterprise. Some continue to do missions but narrow it to the moral endeavor of Christian service to fellow humankind. On the other hand, many who claim to be preserving Christian traditions from history in the name of "evangelicalism" also fail to evaluate their practices theologically. In some places, oppressive missionary thinking relies on the West's socioeconomic and political superiority as a missionary tool. Amid such contrasting attitudes, there certainly are Christians who are persuaded of God's active missionary engagement in the world and who genuinely attempt to be a part of that enterprise. The present work follows this third line of thinking. I do not claim to provide the correct understanding or know how to clean up the mess surrounding Christian missions in history. Rather I attempt to provide a theological lens for the church's missionary calling. If this helps clean the messy missiological house, that will be an added benefit.

2. Martin Kähler, *Schriften zur Christologie und Mission* (Munich: Kaiser, 1971), quoted in David J. Bosch, *Transforming Mission: Paradigm Shifts in Theology of Mission*, 20th anniv. ed. (Maryknoll, NY: Orbis Books, 2011), 16.

We will look at connections between our core Christian beliefs[3] and our missionary thinking to identify the theology of Christian missions. In so doing, we will not discuss much about various practices of missions; our interest is to locate their theological foundation and identify dogmatic themes and thoughts in order to refine missiological thinking.

God's Work in the World and Theology of Mission

In this work, I propose that theology of mission deals with God's work in the world. I assume a belief in God and propose that belief in God's active engagement with the world is the foundation of the theology of mission. Without faith in an active God engaging in the world, I do not believe that we can talk much about the Christian mission. We may differ in our ideas about how and to what extent God is active in the world, but believing that he is at work is essential for mission theology. At two ends of a spectrum are God and the world, and there's a whole lot in between.

While not all aspects of theology are necessarily missiological, our understanding of the theology of mission is broad and general to the extent that some may find it unhelpful. Others may find it unhelpful to talk about mission in this generalized way. We locate the theological foundation of mission in the Trinity, especially in the economic Trinity as made known through the incarnation. The very concept of God as triune is already missiological; the doctrine of the Trinity came about from what we believe to be God's way of working. Trinitarian revival in the twentieth century and an emphasis on the economy of the Trinity are certainly major influences on our project. At the heart of the doctrine of the Trinity, I will argue, is God's mission of salvation through the incarnation. Not only does the doctrine of incarnation lead to the trinitarian formulation, but it is also the foundation of God's salvific economy. We discuss trinitarian theology

3. Roger Olson classifies Christian beliefs into three categories according to their importance: dogma, doctrine, and opinions or interpretations. Most of what we consider here may be classified as dogmas. See Roger E. Olson, *The Story of Christian Theology: Twenty Centuries of Tradition and Reform* (Downers Grove, IL: IVP Academic, 1999), 17–18.

of mission and the incarnation as the way of that mission in chapter 1. The implications of the incarnation for the relationship between gospel and culture will be picked up again in the last chapter (chap. 5).

By dealing with God's economy of salvation, we investigate the goal and task of mission as found in God's salvific work in the world. The topic of salvation, framed as God's missionary engagement, spans the next two chapters (chaps. 2 and 3). Salvation as God's work and salvation as experienced by human beings have often been confused in missiological discussions. While our emphasis is generally on the former, we realize that one cannot really be discussed without the other. In chapter 2, I will lay out some biblical and theoretical motifs of salvation as seen in the history of missiological discussion. With Christology as a focal point, I will end with traditional Western theories of salvation. In chapter 3, I will explore the theoretical discussion in the context of the global church by looking into the dimensions and scope of salvation. I consider the experiential side of salvation to see how salvation has been variously conceived. My aim is to show the richness of the theology of salvation and how its different facets came about to reveal God's mission to save the whole creation. If this approach appears to neglect the context of religious plurality, that is because I deal with theologies of religious plurality in connection with the scope of salvation. My approach of drawing from dialectical oppositions and finding a credible position in the tension—however uncomfortable—will be clearly seen here and in chapter 3.

The missionary response to God's work in the world (or God's mission) is part of the church's witness, making the study of Christian missions an ecclesiological matter. Ecclesiology thrived and made great strides in the ecumenical atmosphere of the twentieth-century church. In this same ecumenical spirit, in chapter 4 I trace different paths in which God's mission featured at the center of ecclesiology. Then I highlight biblical images of the church and their missiological implications.

The last chapter addresses the relationship between gospel and culture. One might think that one of the points I pursue there—namely, the gospel's universality as the foundation of the theology of mission and cultural plurality—should be made in an earlier chapter. However, in the present arrangement, it fits best in the last chapter.

A careful reading of the Bible does not reveal Christian missionary thinking as obviously as we may like. The very hermeneutic we identify in the Bible, I argue, must serve as the basis for our own thinking. We try to capture this principle of interpretation under the rubric of particularity and universality, or as a movement "from one to many." How God has acted in one story, the story of Israel, is how God deals with people of different cultures. By electing and working through one, or the few, such as Abraham and Israel, God reaches all.

Rowan Williams has wittingly defined theological methodology using three characteristics of theology. He says theology is celebratory, communicative, and critical.[4] Using these three Cs, he outlines what a theological methodology should look like. Theology in Christian history begins first as a celebration, evoking visions of glory and celebrating God's sovereignty—rather than arguing about various interpretations. Theology also seeks to communicate in different cultural environments using different tools. Theology deals with faith in God as—in Anselm's famous definition—"faith seeking understanding." The other end of the attempt to understand faith is the goal to explain or communicate that faith. One of the most conspicuous aspects of theology in modern times is its critical nature. This often takes the form of "negative theology," which Williams says, "remains one of the most basic forms of critical theology."[5] Critical theology may move in one of two directions: either toward "agnosticism, even nihilism," or "toward a rediscovery of the celebratory by hinting at the gratuitous mysteriousness of what theology deals with."[6] Thus, I would surmise that any comprehensive theological reflection should involve all three Cs (it should be celebratory, communicative, and critical). However, I would add two more Cs to the list as they apply to the present work: "confessional" and "contextual." Williams may already include "confessional" in his mind under "celebratory," and "contextual" under "communicative," but even so, these two deserve to be spelled out because of their significance in the discussion here.

4. Rowan Williams, *On Christian Theology*, Challenges in Contemporary Theology (Oxford: Blackwell, 2000), xiii.
5. Williams, *On Christian Theology*, xv.
6. Williams, *On Christian Theology*, xv.

On Easter Monday in mid-April 2020, in his daily briefing on the coronavirus outbreak in New York, Governor Andrew Cuomo explained how they had flattened the rising curve of COVID-19 cases in the state. He said, "The number is down because we brought the number down. God did not do that. Fate did not do that. Destiny did not do that."[7] Around the same time, I was browsing the fortieth-anniversary edition of Jürgen Moltmann's book *The Crucified God*, and I could not help contrasting what I heard from Governor Cuomo with what I was reading. What a difference in how we perceive God in relation to the world and God's work in the world. It took me a while to digest the two together and to even make sense of the difference, especially in a pandemic-stricken, politically polarized society where the tendency is to choose one side and thrash the other. I understand Governor Cuomo's words as his way of stressing how important it is for all citizens to do their part in the fight against COVID-19. Even then, the gap between Moltmann's and Cuomo's understandings of God was too wide for me to fill. I understand Moltmann's work to be an invitation to see God in a different way.

I am convinced that this invitation is as urgent today as it was when Moltmann's book was first published almost fifty years ago. His radical work of linking the theology of the cross with the doctrine of the Trinity shows the depth of God's solidarity with humanity in crisis. The resulting theology of passion and God's unfathomable passion became an invitation to see God from a different perspective. Perhaps that is what the present volume can also contribute to the theology of mission, joining the chorus of theological works on Christian missions during the last three decades. In his preface to the paperback edition, Moltmann tells the story of how he conceived *The Crucified God*:

> I saw that when God reveals himself to us godless men and women, who turn ourselves into proud and unhappy gods, he does not do so through power and glory. He reveals himself through suffering and cross, so he repudiates in us the arrogant man or woman and accepts the sinner in us. But then I turned the question around, instead

7. Mario Cuomo, "Clip of New York Governor Cuomo Coronavirus News Conference," user-created clip by AGoerener, C-SPAN, April 13, 2020, https://www.c-span.org/video/?c4868256/user-clip-mario-cuomo.

of asking just *what God means for us human beings* in the cross of Christ, I asked too *what this human cross of Christ means for God*. I found the answer in the idea of God's passion, which reveals itself in the passion of Christ.[8]

Clarification of Key Concepts

Theology and Its Mission

Theology as a concept and as a discipline has been understood and used at different levels. The more basic its level of use, the broader the concept. The more highly specialized the use, the more specific the reference. When used in the broad sense of the term, it often refers to the universally common practice of talking about God. When used in a more specific sense, however, no theology can be seen to be universal. The history of the development of the discipline seems to follow an increasingly specific understanding of theology.

In its most basic and broad sense, "theology" refers to any discourse about God.[9] In recent theological literature, the term "God-talk"[10] has become popular for this meaning of theology. In other contexts, theological references can be so specific that the fundamental sense of theology as a discourse on God is disguised or obscured. Over time, theology has become a disciplinary study of different Christian doctrines in the academic context. From there, the term "theology" has been used to refer to different aspects of Christian faith and beliefs. Theology is a process through which life situations are reflected, deriving specific theological meanings from such situations and contexts. In the modern religious context, "theology" can even mean "an analysis of religious beliefs—even if these beliefs make no reference to god at all."[11] Such a variety of usage has clouded the fundamental meaning of the word.

8. Jürgen Moltmann, *The Crucified God*, 40th anniv. ed. (Minneapolis: Fortress, 2015), xiii (emphasis original).
9. Alister McGrath, *Christian Theology: An Introduction*, 2nd ed. (Oxford: Blackwell, 1997), 142.
10. See, e.g., Veli-Matti Kärkkäinen, *The Doctrine of God: A Global Introduction* (Grand Rapids: Baker Academic, 2004), 8–10.
11. McGrath, *Christian Theology: An Introduction*, 142.

Locating theology of mission in the range of theological disciplines can also be difficult because the concept of mission itself is multidimensional. A helpful approach is to see God and his mission (*missio Dei*) as a starting point for understanding theology. And so we understand theology basically as a discourse about God and his works. The word "theology" was used in this sense, says Alister McGrath, "as systematic analysis of the nature, purpose, and activity of God."[12] By returning to this basic understanding of theology as a study of God's nature and activity, we reflect on the identity and meaning of theology of mission.

This approach to look first into the nature of God and his work objectively as the heart of theology operates with certain assumptions. First, before one can ever talk about God as the object of one's faith, one must recognize that faith is inherently subjective. Before treating God and God's work as the object of our faith, we need to acknowledge that we are dealing with our belief, a very subjective matter. The very process of possessing a particular faith in God is itself a theological process. Yet because our goal here is to clarify an area of theology—namely, mission theology—we can do no more than acknowledge this subjectivity so that we may focus attention on the object of that faith. While it is right to state that Christian theology begins with the Christian faith, it is also true that the source of this faith is God himself. Our belief that God is triune and our faith in the Second Person (Christology) and Third Person (pneumatology) of the Trinity serve as the source as well as the objects of our faith. A second assumption of our approach is that it does not and cannot negate the complexity of theology, which has been systematized into subdisciplines. Each area of inquiry, including soteriology (theology of salvation) and ecclesiology (theology of the church), is complex and depends on faith in God and God's work, as will be dealt with in later chapters.

God in a Global Religious Context

The fact that we translate what we commonly call "God" from one language to another shows the existence of some commonality

---

12. McGrath, *Christian Theology: An Introduction*, 142.

in the concept. This, of course, is not to say that the meanings we
attribute to God are necessarily the same. Even when the same terms
are used, their meanings and usage can be very different.[13] Even within
Christianity, a compilation of theologians' work shows quite diverse
approaches to and emphases on the idea of God.[14] Recent discourses
on God at various levels have brought out rich and diverse aspects of
an understanding of God. The growing proximity among people of
different nations, regions, cultures, and religions has impacted our
conceptions in many ways. While this globalizing development has a
homogenizing tendency, it also increasingly honors particular ways
of conceiving of God or Gods. Through daily conversations in our
world, people of different religions are not only learning from one
another but also influencing how other people think of God. Between
those who call themselves "theocentric" in their studies of other religions and those who strictly reflect on the Christian monotheistic
concept of God, discourses on a God-concept along spatial, cultural,
and religious lines have enriched the Christian God-concept in various
ways. Because of the stress we place on God in the theology of Christian mission in this book, it will be helpful to locate the Christian
conception of it in the global religious context.

Different religious persuasions conceive of God, as well as God's
locale and level of activities, differently. Such variances also exist
among members of the same religious group. While it is quite possible
to argue that religious views influence one's concept of God, it is also
possible that one's God-concept (or its equivalent, such as Supreme
Being, the Absolute, the absolute Path or Paths, or Supreme Power)
serves and directs religious conceptions. Theology revolves around
the conception of God and is best understood if we start there, or
with equivalent conceptions such as the absolute truths and paths
in Buddhism.

13. Timothy Tennent, for instance, deals with the use of the Arabic "Allah" in
Judeo-Christian and Muslim traditions as a reference to the one God. He concludes
that Muslims changed the use of the term from a general reference in the pre-Islamic
Jewish and Christian faith to a personalized name for God. Previously, "Allah" was
equivalent to 'el or *theos*, but in its Muslim meaning, it became equivalent to the
Jewish "Yahweh." See Timothy Tennent, *Theology in the Context of World Christianity* (Grand Rapids: Zondervan, 2007), 25–49.
    14. See Kärkkäinen, *Doctrine of God*.

Friedrich Heiler has been credited with pioneering a popular classification of the world's religions into two major types: prophetic (Semitic) and mystic (Indian). Keith Ward nuances Heiler's work by first identifying four groups of religions according to their "central focal concepts," representing "four different images of the Supreme Power and Value of Being."[15] He calls them "the Semitic Judge of the World, the Greek Logos, the Indian desireless Self, and the Chinese cosmic harmony."[16] This characterization of different religious conceptions of God or Gods helps our purpose to locate Christian faith in God within world religions. The Christian conception of God has two sources in this list—namely, the Semitic Judge of the world and the Greek Logos. Ward further consolidates these four into Heiler's two groups of Semitic "prophetic" religions and Indo-Asian "mystics" because "the Greek and Chinese images have been absorbed into the Semitic and Indian, though in the process they have changed the characters of their host traditions."[17] Indian theologian M. M. Thomas renames Heiler's prophetic religions and mystics as "Messianic" and "Unitive" and offers the following explanation: "The broad division is between the Judeo-Christian-Islamic traditions which take history as the fundamental sphere of the self-revelation and saving action of God, and the other religions of African, Indian, and Chinese origins which see salvation in the enduring vision of an undifferentiated spiritual unity or harmony of nature, man, spirits, and gods."[18]

One can see that these attempts to simplify world religions by classifying them into two groups need substantial qualification. Many feel that placing primal religions in general and African traditional religions in particular together with Indian and Chinese religions is at best inappropriate and at worst marginalizing. Including the highly complex philosophical religions of Confucianism and Taoism with Indian mystical religion seems unfair and unfounded. However, even these broad generalizations reveal some common characteristics between the two groups. For the present work, this generalized

---

15. Keith Ward, *Religion and Revelation: A Theology of Revelation in the World's Religions* (Oxford: Oxford University Press, 1994), 95.

16. Ward, *Religion and Revelation*, 95.

17. Ward, *Religion and Revelation*, 95.

18. M. M. Thomas, *Man and the Universe of Faiths* (Madras, India: Diocesan Press 1975), 33–34.

classification is helpful for locating the complex conception of the Christian triune God.

Between the prophetic and the unitive types of religions, we see some significantly different ways of understanding God/Gods or the divine. Today, the prophetic religions are largely clustered under the Abrahamic faith traditions, and the unitive group consists of Indian and East Asian religions. Keith Ward makes some crucial observations on the differences between the prophetic (or Semitic) and unitive (as found in Vedic) traditions: "In the Semitic tradition, a succession of prophets was possessed by the Word of God, who was experienced as absolute moral demand, judge of all human conduct. Their visions were of a personal God who demanded justice and mercy. The Divine power was experienced in historical acts of deliverance from oppression. Thus arose the concept of the suprasensory as ultimately unified in a dynamic power which relates to the imperfect present as judge and deliverer. The idea of God became that of one personal, active, and transcendent being with a moral goal for the universe."[19]

The final sentence of this quotation summarizing God as a "personal, active, and transcendent being with a moral goal for the universe" is a crucial description of the tradition. Ward contrasts this vision with the traditions surrounding Vedic religious visions that came out of India. About these traditions, in comparison to the Semitic tradition, he says, "There were no prophets who felt challenged by a morally judging God and who issued condemnation on oppressive social systems. There was no development of belief in a historical purpose or goal. And there was little sense of one creator who stood apart from creation, as a being quite different in kind, except in later, largely heterodox, traditions like Sikhism."[20]

The contrast helps to show the distinctiveness of the God-concept in the Abrahamic faith tradition within which the Christian trinitarian God is further distinguished. Ward further comments on how the different conditions of the people impacted their conception of God. Whereas the Israelites were nomads in search of a home and were delivered from slavery to freedom, Indians of Vedic tradition were not

19. Ward, *Religion and Revelation*, 134.
20. Ward, *Religion and Revelation*, 135.

slaves seeking a home but were "conquerors seeking to dominate a continent of immense and fertile space."[21] Thus, "their gods or devas (spirit-powers) took over and took up residence in a vast continent where the cycles of nature seemed to be rich and endless."[22] The Gods are not figures of moral commands nor liberating ones. Instead, they affirm the status quo and build their religious teachings from there. Although social conditions and existence do not necessarily create God in the human image, they do seem to affect how we conceive of God's attributes and character.

On Being Global in Context

In speaking of the global church or perspective, I do not mean globalization as used in connection with the capitalist-driven market economy. Rather, I intend to be as inclusively global as possible in the theological conversation that follows. As I have shown elsewhere, I consider world Christianity to be in a transitional stage.[23] While most people groups of the majority world (or non-Western world) have diverse characteristics, their commonality has primarily been their being "non-West." We cannot deny the fact that we continue to classify nations of the world as West or non-West. This means the West continues to define how things work in the world. Without endorsing this classification, we recognize it as the present condition of global existence. It is what it is.

In this global context, the enterprise of theological construction is caught between Western and non-Western. Unfortunately, many theologies in the non-Western world are still constructed in response to Western theology. In this transitional period, Christians of different traditions in the majority (non-Western) world are making substantial efforts to construct relevant theologies for and from their contexts. The changing nature of theology is still largely visible in these new emerging theological works. The most dominant voices behind these new theological writings have various responses or reactions to Western theologies. While an increasing number have good

21. Ward, *Religion and Revelation*, 135–36.
22. Ward, *Religion and Revelation*, 136.
23. Lalsangkima Pachuau, *World Christianity: A Historical and Theological Introduction* (Nashville: Abingdon, 2018), 16–21.

14

God at Work in the World

theological substance, many have little or no contextual theological substance. Such works that dominated among non-Western theological voices until the recent past may be categorized under three types. Let me call them the "naysayers," the "need-sayers," and the "nonsayers," according to their responses to Western Christianity and theologies.

The "naysayers" are radical reactionary voices so occupied with saying "no" to Western Christianity and theologies that they end up saying little or nothing of substance on their own theology. In many cases, the attempt is so anti-Western that criticism becomes the overriding theme. The "need-sayers" are those who primarily use their work to describe the need for a new theology from non-Western contexts. So far, this is the category with the greatest number of works. The "nonsayers" are those who neither refute Western theology nor see the need to construct contextual theologies. They accept Western theology uncritically as the authority. While this position may still be common among lay Christians without theological training, it is decreasing considerably among those who are theologically educated. Needless to say, we are in a transitional period in theology.

It may be wishful to think that we can move away from constructing theology between the West and the non-West into a truly world-inclusive global theological construction. However, that is what we need. Such a global theological construction can arise out of a spirit that recognizes we all are a part of the world, a world larger than each of us, each region, and our sociocultural categories. The concept of contextual theology came out of the majority world as thinkers in those regions moved from Western-dominated theology into theologizing in their contexts. Western theology that once saw itself as the universal theology is increasingly recognizing the voices of the non-Western majority world. A truly inclusive world for theology requires us to recognize that we are each part of the whole and that each theology is a contextual theology.[24] I think—and indeed hope—this is what we are beginning to see in contextual theological works. Changing its self-perception from being the dominant figure to being

24. As Douglas John Hall rightly says, "No theological province of the *oikoumēnē* can be independent of the others." See Douglas John Hall, *Thinking the Faith: Christian Theology in a North American Context* (Minneapolis: Fortress, 1991), 21.

a part of the larger whole is a humbling experience for the West. With this recognition, we should also not shy away from claiming the world as our own larger context.

Context is always multilayered. At each layer, we share common traits with others. We can imagine these layers with our immediate context at the bottom and our commonality as human beings in one world at the top. We do not need to peel off upper layers to reach lower layers. We own them together and use them according to our needs. Our theological constructs may follow a similar pattern. Theology can be done in a very particular context as well as in a more general context. The particular ones are not authenticated by eliminating the more general ones. We all share a global context, and we all have our own local contexts.

Contextual theology can be and should be done at different levels of contexts. Limiting it to one level may make theology inauthentic. The different contexts we share with others make us who we are. If we let our different contexts compete and conflict, we will only destroy ourselves. Instead of disclaiming some in order to claim others, we must own them all. Each has a part in and of us. The West has become a part of my context, although it may never be the same context that it is for my American colleagues. A context is not an isolated, autonomous entity; it is always dynamic and related to other contexts. As the world becomes increasingly global, we each change our frame of reference, even our self-perceptions. We all seem to have written ourselves into the larger contexts in our world.

This book does not pretend to be an exhaustive study of the different aspects of the theology of mission, nor is it a comprehensive guide for the topic. Rather, it is more like a pathway. I understand my work to be like clearing a pathway in the thick jungle of theological thoughts. The work by necessity is interdisciplinary within the field of theological studies. I do not pretend to know the authorities in different areas of study nor do I intend to compile a selection of helpful resources. I try to pave the way as I see it, having a theology of mission as both my approach and my goal. By "theology of mission," I simply mean the missionary dimension in understanding God, as such an understanding has been passed down through the tradition of theological discussions.

By saying that I am the one paving the way, I do not mean that I construct the way, and thus all new ideas come from me. Everything I do is because of the rich body of knowledge that informs me. I pick and choose my theological interlocutors, partners in dialogue, and sources, which help me take the needed twists and turns for a probable and reasonable way. I try to be honest in referring to the sources that have influenced my thinking, but I cannot name them all. There are far too many voices and thoughts that have led me to think as I do. If I confess my biases, they are my bent toward historical-theological study and my inclination toward biblical textual studies. These will become apparent in what follows.

1

THE TRIUNE GOD IN MISSION

Trinitarian Theology and the Mission of God

The tumultuous twentieth century brought a major crisis to the missionary world, while also stimulating new thinking about the nature of missions. Theology was the recourse for missionary thinkers in the 1950s grappling with the challenges created by the changing world political order. A statement from the International Missionary Council's meeting in 1952 reads, "The missionary movement of which we are a part has its source in the Triune God himself."[1] A game-changing concept of *missio Dei* (God's mission) ensued, resulting in a new theology of mission. In this chapter, we combine the theology of *missio Dei* with the revival of theological study of the Trinity in recent decades. By doing so, we focus our attention on the incarnation of Christ as the channel of God's mission in the power of the Holy Spirit. We also assume basic knowledge of the doctrines of the Trinity and Christology. In their historical formation, the two are intertwined in that the discernment of Christ's divinity led to

---

1. International Missionary Council, *The Missionary Obligation of the Church, Willingen, Germany, July 5–17, 1952* (London: Edinburgh House, 1952), 2.

the formation of the doctrine of the Trinity in the fourth and fifth centuries.[2]

We begin by discussing the trinitarian inquiry from the latter part of the twentieth century and then consider how the theology of the Trinity relates to the theology of mission based on the *missio Dei* concept. Dynamic ecumenical conversations today provide a conducive framework for the missiological meaning of the Trinity. Asians' engagements with the doctrine of the Trinity in their cultural and religious pluralistic contexts further exemplify its richness in missionary contexts. To relate the theology of the Trinity with the missionary enterprise, we trace the use of the word "mission" in the trinitarian theology of Aquinas in relation to the introduction of the modern concept of "missions" by Ignatius Loyola and the Jesuits. As much as there are significant lessons to be drawn from Aquinas's theology, the meaning of "missions" reaches the church in practice through the missionary endeavor initiated by Ignatius.

Following the discussion of Aquinas's divine mission of the economic Trinity, the chapter proposes the economy of salvation as the task of the divine mission of the Son and the Spirit. Trinitarian theology has its missiological significance through the doctrine of Christ's incarnation and its salvific goal. The chapter ends by considering the incarnation as the way and means of achieving God's mission in the world. God's entrance into human history in Christ and his full identification with humanity have important implications in the gospel-culture relation that we will trace in chapter 5.

Trinitarian Theology Today

The last quarter of the twentieth century saw a renaissance of trinitarian theology, which was both energizing and innovative. These discussions reshaped the theology with strong critiques of some traditional conceptions of the doctrine. In the few centuries prior, trinitarian theology was largely muted in Western theological literature. Post-Enlightenment modern theology treated the doctrine with sus-

---

2. For a recent study on the history of trinitarian doctrine, see Khaled Anatolios, *Retrieving Nicaea: The Development and Meaning of Trinitarian Doctrine* (Grand Rapids: Baker Academic, 2011).

picion. For some, such as Immanuel Kant, the doctrine was at best unwarranted and at worst pointless: "The doctrine of the Trinity, taken literally, has no practical relevance at all, even if we think we understand it, and it is even more clearly irrelevant if we realize that it transcends all our concepts."[3] The dogma of the Trinity, in the words of Paul Tillich, "became an impenetrable mystery, put on the altar, to be adored. And the mystery ceased to be the eternal mystery of the ground of being; it became instead the riddle of an unsolved theological problem and in many cases, . . . the glorification of an absurdity in numbers."[4] Thus, modern theology in the West largely avoided the doctrine of the Trinity without entirely discarding it. Beginning with the work of Karl Barth in the 1930s and enhanced by Karl Rahner in the 1960s and 1970s, the doctrine has been revived and is being reestablished as foundational to the enterprise of theology.

Keith Johnson helpfully points out that the doctrine of the Trinity provided Karl Barth the much-needed resources to overcome his struggle "with the question of how humans can know God without shaping this knowledge according to the confines of human subjectivity."[5] As a way of combating the post-Kantian suspicion of the human ability to know God, Barth locates trinitarian theology, or all theology for that matter, within the realm of God's revelation. He insists that "revelation is the basis of the doctrine of the Trinity; the doctrine of the Trinity has no other basis apart from this."[6] In this, Barth starts at the divine economy of self-revelation and somewhat reverses the traditional approach, which begins with the ontological Trinity. Yet, he insists that the revealed, the revelation, and the revealer cannot be distinguished from one another: "According to Scripture, God's

3. Immanuel Kant, *The Conflict of the Faculties*, trans. Mary J. Gregor (New York: Abaris Books, 1979), 65, quoted in Thomas R. Thompson, "Trinitarianism Today: Doctrinal Renaissance, Ethical Relevance, Social Redolence," *Calvin Theological Journal* 32 (1997): 9.

4. Paul Tillich, *Systematic Theology*, vol. 3, *Life and the Spirit, History and the Kingdom of God* (Chicago: University of Chicago Press, 1963), 291.

5. Keith L. Johnson, *The Essential Karl Barth: A Reader and Commentary* (Grand Rapids: Baker Academic, 2019), 127. Johnson's point relates to the epistemological problem posed by Kantian philosophy, which limits the possibility of trinitarian theology.

6. Karl Barth, *Church Dogmatics* I/1 (Edinburgh: T&T Clark, 1975), 304, quoted in Johnson, *Essential Karl Barth*, 129.

revelation is God's own direct speech which is not to be distinguished from the act of speaking and therefore is not to be distinguished from God himself, from the divine I which confronts man in this act in which it says Thou to him. Revelation is God speaking in person."[7] Barth's most revolutionary point in this regard is that the God we meet in his revelation (in his economy) is God in his own being (immanent). The God who is wholly other is the God who reveals himself in three modes. "By the doctrine of the Trinity," Barth states, "we understand the Church doctrine of the unity of God in the three modes of being of Father, Son and Holy Ghost, or of the threefold otherness of the one God in the three modes of being of Father, Son and Holy Ghost."[8]

Barth's thoughts on subordinationism and modalism have been debated. While the debates show problems in Barth's trinitarian theology, they also "highlight," to use Kevin Giles's words, "Barth's innovative and mind-expanding understanding of the triune God who is high and humble . . . at the same time."[9] For Barth, according to Johnson, "It is God who reveals Himself equally as the Father in His self-veiling and holiness, as the Son in His self-unveiling and mercy, and as the Spirit in His self-impartation and love. Father, Son, and Spirit are the one, single, and equal God."[10] His explanation of the doctrine serves as a corrective to the separation of immanent Trinity from economic Trinity, a common approach in Western theology since Thomas Aquinas. Barth scholars unanimously affirm that for Barth "God's immanent triunity is known only by way of God's economic triunity,"[11] as "God's being and act are inseparable."[12] In

7. Barth, *Church Dogmatics* I/1, 304, quoted in Johnson, *Essential Karl Barth*, 127.

8. Barth, *Church Dogmatics* I/1, 381, quoted in Johnson, *Essential Karl Barth*, 133. Johnson notes (129n6) that Barth prefers "modes of being" to "person" as the latter "leads to the erroneous notion that the Trinity is the union of three distinct individuals."

9. Kevin Giles, "Barth and Subordinationism," *Scottish Journal of Theology* 64, no. 3 (2011): 327.

10. Johnson, *Essential Karl Barth*, 133.

11. Kevin W. Hector, "God's Triunity and Self-Determination: A Conversation with Karl Barth, Bruce McCormack, and Paul Molnar," *International Journal of Systematic Theology* 7, no. 3 (July 2005): 246.

12. George Hunsinger, "Election and the Trinity: Twenty-Five Theses on the Theology of Karl Barth," *Modern Theology* 24, no. 2 (April 2008): 180.

the words of John Flett, for Barth "God is who he is in his act."[13] As Chung-Hyun Baik argues, from Barth forward, ontology and epistemology became "intricately woven into . . . [the] discussion of the immanent-economic Trinity relation."[14] In the post-Kantian modern theological context, this came as a theological revolution, defying Kantian epistemology and revising much of Western trinitarian discussion. It also gave new reason and a new resource to ponder the theology of the Trinity.

Contemporary interest and debate on trinitarian theology accelerated with the 1967 publication of *The Trinity* by Karl Rahner, one of the most prominent Catholic theologians of the twentieth century. What Barth's theology may have hinted an opposition to, Rahner clearly exposes and squarely opposes—namely, the separation and sequencing of the oneness and the triunity of God. He observes this separation and sequencing in Thomas Aquinas's treatises *On the One God* and *On the Triune God*, and he opines that such a separation may be derived from Augustine.[15] This separation and sequencing led to the separation and distancing of the immanent, or ontological, Trinity ("who and what kind of being God is in himself")[16] from the economic, or historical, Trinity ("the threefold way in which God is known to us and works out our salvation").[17] In such "separation and sequence," Rahner charges, "the unity and connection of the two treatises are easily overlooked, as evidenced by the very fact that this separation and sequence are considered quite naturally as necessary and obvious."[18] By contrast, Rahner's basic thesis is captured in his now-famous axiom: "The 'economic' Trinity is the 'immanent' Trinity and the 'immanent' Trinity is the

13. John G. Flett, *The Witness of God: The Trinity, Missio Dei, Karl Barth, and the Nature of Christian Community* (Grand Rapids: Eerdmans, 2010), 2.

14. Chung-Hyun Baik, "A Matrix of Ontology, Epistemology, and Mystery in Karl Barth and Karl Rahner on the Immanent-Economic Trinity Relation," *Theology Today* 75, no. 3 (2018): 297–317.

15. Karl Rahner, *The Trinity*, trans. Joseph Donceel (New York: Herder and Herder, 1970), 16–17. The original German version of the book was published in 1967.

16. Colin E. Gunton, *The Promise of Trinitarian Theology*, 2nd ed. (Edinburgh: T&T Clark, 1997), xvii.

17. William C. Placher, *The Triune God: An Essay in Postliberal Theology* (Louisville: Westminster John Knox, 2007), 138.

18. Rahner, *Trinity*, 20.

'economic' Trinity."[19] Rahner builds his defense around the incarnation and argues "that no adequate distinction can be made between the doctrine of the Trinity and the doctrine of the economy
of salvation."[20]

The origin of the classification of the "immanent" and "economic"
Trinity goes back to the distinction of *theologia* and *oikonomia* made
by the church fathers. *Theologia* (theology) "refers to the mystery of
God's inmost life within the Blessed Trinity" and *oikonomia* (economy) "to all the works by which God reveals himself and communicates his life," explains the *Catechism of the Catholic Church*.[21] In
its simplest terms, immanent Trinity refers to "God in Godself," and
economic Trinity refers to "God for us."[22] Although some credit Aquinas for the nomenclature, his contribution was on the concept and not
on the terms themselves.[23] According to Gilles Emery, "St. Thomas
distinguishes 'immanent' action, which remains in the acting subject,
and 'transitive' action, which transmitted to a reality outside the acting subject. This explanation, which is not the only one, contains the
fundamental principles of Thomas' reflection on what we today call
the 'immanent Trinity' and the 'economic Trinity.'"[24] There are some
criticisms of this distinction. Fred Sanders, for instance, opines that the
terms may create more confusion than clarity.[25] Catherine LaCugna
makes her case that the distinction which originated in *oikonomia* and

---

19. Rahner, *Trinity*, 22 (emphasis original).

20. Rahner, *Trinity*, 24.

21. Catholic Church, *Catechism of the Catholic Church*, 2nd ed. (Vatican: Libreria
Editrice Vaticana, 2000), 62.

22. Chung-Hyun Baik titled his book *The Holy Trinity—God for God and God
for Us: Seven Positions on the Immanent-Economic Trinity Relation in Contemporary
Trinitarian Theology* (Eugene, OR: Pickwick, 2011). In his review of the book, James
Gordon appropriately rephrases the title as "God for Godself and God for Us." See
James Gordon, review of *The Holy Trinity—God for God and God for Us: Seven
Positions on the Immanent-Economic Trinity Relation in Contemporary Trinitarian
Theology* by Chung-Hyun Baik, *International Journal of Systematic Theology* 17,
no. 4 (October, 2015): 484–88.

23. According to Wolfhart Pannenberg, the precise terminology comes from Jo-
hann Augustus Urlsperger (1728–1806). See Pannenberg, *Systematic Theology*, trans.
Geoffrey W. Bromiley (Grand Rapids: Eerdmans, 1991), 1:291n111.

24. Gilles Emery, *The Trinitarian Theology of St Thomas Aquinas*, trans. Fran-
cesca Aran Murphy (Oxford: Oxford University Press, 2007), 41.

25. Fred Sanders, "What Is the Economic and Immanent Trinity?," *ZA Blog*,
Zondervan Academic, April 27, 2018, https://zondervanacademic.com/blog/what-is

theologia and the importance given to the latter have largely led to the "defeat" of the doctrine of the Trinity.[26] She rejects the immanent-economic distinction and upholds the *oikonomia-theologia* relationship, as in the inseparability of soteriology and theology.[27] As we will make clear later, the distinction—whether *oikonomia* and *theologia* or economic and immanent—is helpful for the purpose of locating the theology of mission within the broad scope of theology. LaCugna's interpretation of the Trinity as a "practical doctrine,"[28] which is often seen as leaning toward the economic Trinity,[29] is where we will locate theology of mission. Theology of mission is best understood as focusing on the practical aspect of trinitarian theology, especially as it relates to God's economy of salvation.

Neither Rahner nor Barth eliminates the ontological inquiry of God *in esse* (in his being or immanence), but both assert that such an inquiry cannot be made apart from God's self-revelation (in Rahner's terms, "self-communication"). Both insist that the inquiry begins with God's self-revelation or communication—thus the economic Trinity. In fact, this is how Rahner arrives at the immanent Trinity: "The differentiation of the self-communication of God in history (of truth) and spirit (of love) must belong to God 'in himself,' or otherwise this difference, which undoubtedly exists, would do away with God's self-communication."[30] He further explains, "There is real difference in God as he is in himself between one and the same God as he is . . . the unoriginated who mediates himself to himself (Father), the one who is in truth uttered for himself (Son), and the one who is received and accepted in love for himself (Spirit)."[31] The "bond" between the "self-communicator [Father] and the one who

-the-economic-and-immanent-trinity. For Sanders's broader argument, see his *The Triune God* (Grand Rapids: Zondervan, 2016).

26. Catherine Mowry LaCugna, *God for Us: The Trinity and Christian Life* (New York: HarperCollins, 1991), 9. LaCugna traces the history of the doctrine in the East and the West to the end of the medieval church and calls it "the emergence and defeat of the doctrine of the Trinity."

27. See Elizabeth Groppe, "Catherine Mowry LaCugna's Contribution to Trinitarian Theology," *Theological Studies* 63 (2002): 730–63.

28. LaCugna, *God for Us*, 1.

29. Groppe, "Catherine Mowry LaCugna's Contribution," 741–42.

30. Rahner, *Trinity*, 99–100.

31. Rahner, *Trinity*, 101–2.

is uttered [Son] and received [Spirit] . . . must be understood as 'relative' (relational)."[32]

Rahner's and Barth's calls for the unity of the immanent and economic Trinity ignited new interest and paved new pathways to consider trinitarian theology. Vibrant debates and engagements among theologians on various aspects of trinitarian theology have produced a rich theological discussion. One particular line of thought, imprecisely associated with the rubric of "social trinitarianism,"[33] has produced one of the most creative and productive interpretations. Theologians like Protestant Jürgen Moltmann and Eastern Orthodox John Zizioulas[34] highlight the relational aspect within the divine persons in the Trinity and draw implications for ecclesial and sociopolitical practices. Some of these interpretations have been made in contradistinction from the so-called Latin interpretation, which derives from the work of Augustine of Hippo. While these differing viewpoints can be polarizing at some level, their engaging dialogues also greatly enrich the theology.

One of the most significant developments is the ecumenical conversations and resourcing of the theology, especially across the different confessional bodies. From Eastern Orthodox to Roman Catholic and Protestant, today's trinitarian theology draws from all traditions, including evangelical and Pentecostal-charismatic traditions. As shown in the works of scholars such as Jürgen Moltmann, John Zizioulas, Catherine LaCugna, Robert Jenson, Wolfhart Pannenberg, and Colin Gunton, the new ecumenical reading has yielded dynamic ways of engaging trinitarian theology. Comprehensive yet creative thinking such as Jenson's has spurred further engagements and thought.[35] As Gunton helpfully highlights, the immanent-economic debate is central to

32. Rahner, *Trinity*, 102.

33. For a critical and analytical explanation and assessment of social trinitarianism and its critics, see Gijsbert van den Brink, "Social Trinitarianism: A Discussion of Some Recent Theological Criticisms," *International Journal of Systematic Theology* 16, no. 3 (July 2014): 331–50.

34. John Zizioulas, *Being as Communion: Studies in Personhood and the Church* (London: Darton, Longman & Todd, 1985).

35. For a good discussion on Jenson's work and its influences, see Colin E. Gunton, ed., *Trinity, Time, and Church: A Response to the Theology of Robert W. Jenson* (Grand Rapids: Eerdmans, 2000).

the conversation today. On one end of the spectrum are those who advocate the economic Trinity for the purpose of being "concretely relevant," and on the opposite end are those who seek "to validate" the doctrine mainly or solely "on the basis of . . . the immanent or ontological Trinity."[36] Gunton warned of "over-simplification" and "superficiality"[37] on both sides.

The impact of the trinitarian renaissance is felt in different fields of theological study. The impact is felt strongly, for instance, in ecclesiological and theological studies of religions. As we will discuss in chapter 4, trinitarian theology spurred new interests and renewal of ecclesial thoughts. Quite distinct from the current discussions in the West highlighted above are creative reflections by Asian thinkers in their multireligious contexts. Simon Chan convincingly shows that the concept of the Trinity poses a serious challenge to Asians. The challenging aspects, he says, include the Judeo-Christian understanding of a personal God. Yet, for many Asians, that is also the attraction.[38] Against the Western Protestant egalitarian interpretation of the divine persons, Chan notes that Asians, especially of Confucian and Taoist background, come closer to the traditional Orthodox and Catholic concept of the monarchy of the Father in the Trinity.[39]

Asian theologians have also skillfully interpreted the doctrine of the Trinity in their multireligious context. One of the most imaginative and original Asian thinkers, Raimundo Panikkar, made a deep, meditative, and interreligious exploration of the doctrine in the early 1970s. As the title of his book *The Trinity and the Religious Experience of Man* suggests, Panikkar universalizes Christian faith through a meditation on the Trinity using "the deep intuitions of Hinduism and Buddhism"[40] and arrives at a universal theandric (God-human experience) spirituality.[41] Presenting the Trinity more as a means than an end, Panikkar argues that the Trinity is "a junction where the authentic

36. Gunton, *Promise of Trinitarian Theology*, xvii–xxi.
37. Gunton, *Promise of Trinitarian Theology*, xvii.
38. Simon Chan, *Grassroots Asian Theology: Thinking the Faith from the Ground Up* (Downers Grove, IL: IVP Academic, 2014), 65–66.
39. Chan, *Grassroots Asian Theology*, 66–67.
40. Raimundo Panikkar, *The Trinity and the Religious Experience of Man* (New York: Orbis Books, 1973), 46.
41. Panikkar, *Trinity and the Religious Experience*, 71.

spiritual dimensions of all religions meet."[42] From an East Asian Taoist perspective, Jung Young Lee proposes that the East Asian yin-yang philosophy be used to consider the Trinity, saying that yin-yang thinking is "nondualistic, relational, and complementary." Because of this, God's threeness and oneness are not contradictory for East Asians.[43] Just as the yin-yang philosophy prioritizes wholeness through connection, Lee asserts that one major contribution of the East Asian trinitarian perspective, unlike the Western emphasis on the "substantial," is its relative, inclusive, and above all, holistic framework.[44]

What seem most pertinent to Asians, some recent Asian thinkers suggest, are the familial relationships that the Bible projects with figures such as Father and Son. In much of South and East Asia, where the family is the most basic unit of life and familial relations are considered essential to life, "the Trinity as the divine family takes on a special significance,"[45] says Simon Chan. Some East Asian theologians explore familial relations quite well as a way of understanding the Trinity. George Capaque proposes to use "family structure and experience as a lens to re-envision the Trinity" in the Philippine context.[46] He is, however, careful not to project the human family on the divine but sees the divine family as the archetype of the human family. In the Confucian-influenced worldview where filial piety is obligatory, the Trinity as the divine family makes good sense. The family image is what leads Lee to reclaim "the feminine nature of the Spirit as the image of the mother in the Trinitarian family."[47] Musung Jung of Korea uses filial piety as a way to connect and interpret the concept of *missio Dei* and calls for a *pareo Dei* or "the obeying of God," claiming Jesus is "the filial Son par excellence."[48]

42. Panikkar, *Trinity and the Religious Experience*, 42.

43. Jung Young Lee, *The Trinity in Asian Perspective* (Nashville: Abingdon, 1996), 213.

44. Lee, *Trinity in Asian Perspective*, 213.

45. Chan, *Grassroots Asian Theology*, 66.

46. George N. Capaque, "The Trinity in Asian Contexts," in *Asian Christian Theology: Evangelical Perspectives*, ed. Timoteo D. Gener and Stephen T. Pardue (Carlisle: Langham Global Library, 2019), 75.

47. Lee, *Trinity in Asian Perspective*, 216.

48. Musung Jung, "Toward a Theology of *Pareo Dei*: Exploring a Theology of *Missio Dei* for the Missiological Reconciliation of the Korean Protestant Church" (PhD diss., Asbury Theological Seminary, 2012), 243.

"What makes the current Trinitarian renaissance more than just some reassertion of confessional orthodoxy," observes Thomas Thompson, "is the confidence with which Trinitarians are applying the doctrine to all areas of theological thought."[49] Efforts to ground different themes, approaches, and fields of theological inquiry in the doctrine of Trinity have multiplied during the last few decades—contending approaches from "Latin Trinity" to "Social Trinity,"[50] from feminist theology to public theology, and from ecclesiology to theological ethics and theology of religions.

Trinitarian theology has had especially vibrant results in reconsidering the field of theology of mission. The turn to the economic Trinity as a point of entry to the theological discussion has provided new avenues for developing a solid trinitarian theology of mission. While a few important works have come out, the field is ripe with potential for further exploration. The dynamism of the current trinitarian renaissance has laid important groundwork. Gunton underscores one significant line of thinking, what he calls "the apologetic or missionary function" of the trinitarian theology. Against a common Western notion that trinitarian theology is "of edificatory value" for Christians but is likely a "barrier to belief" for non-Christians, Gunton states that "because the theology of the Trinity has so much to teach about the nature of our world and life within it, it is or could be the centre of Christianity's appeal to the unbeliever, as the good news of a God who enters into free relations of creation and redemption with his world."[51]

In fact, unbeknownst to Western thinkers, trinitarian theology has served as a key point of contact with much of Hindu thought in Indian theological works from the late nineteenth century. We can refer to the creative works of theologians such as Keshub Chander

49. Thompson, "Trinitarianism Today," 12.

50. See, e.g., Norman Metzler, "The Trinity in Contemporary Theology: Questioning the Social Trinity," *Concordia Theological Quarterly* 67, nos. 3–4 (July–October 2003): 270–87; Matthew Zaro Fisher, "A Subservient Trinity: An Alternative to Latin and Social Trinitarian Theories," *The Heythrop Journal* 57 (2016): 964–73; Cornelius Plantinga Jr., "Social Trinity and Tritheism," and Brian Leftow, "A Latin Trinity," in *A Reader in Contemporary Philosophical Theology*, ed. Oliver Crisp (London: T&T Clark, 2009): 65–125.

51. Gunton, *Promise of Trinitarian Theology*, 7.

Sen and Brahmabandhab Upadhyay, who were already relating Trinity with Satchitananda (or *Saccidānanda*) in the late nineteenth and early twentieth centuries. While Sen, whom we might call a non-Christian theologian of Christianity, first proposes the idea, it is Upadhyay who gives the most detailed interpretation.[52] The term *Saccidānanda* appears in later Upanishadic texts to summarize the Upanishad's teaching of Brahman, the Absolute, independent of and unrelated to (or beyond what can be related by) creation. It consists of three components and teaches the Absolute (Brahman) as "being" (*sat*), "consciousness" (*chit*), and "bliss" or joy (*ananda*). Brahmabandhab Upadhyay carefully interprets each to express his Indian Advaitic understanding of the Trinity, "the very nature of God as one essence possessed undividedly by Three Persons."[53] But it is not only in the intellectual philosophical realm that the Trinity appeals to Hindus. Lesslie Newbigin, former missionary-bishop in India, reports that the Trinity provided a starting point for simple Indian evangelists preaching in villages.[54]

Missio Dei *and the Christian Missionary Enterprise*

The introduction and development of the concept of *missio Dei* (God's mission) has become a common narrative in the twentieth-century history of missions.[55] For our purpose here, we will provide a brief summary of the development. The first person to use *missio Dei* in connection with the modern missionary enterprise was Karl Hartenstein in the 1930s. However, it wasn't until after the Inter-

52. Timothy C. Tennent, *Building Christianity on Indian Foundations: The Legacy of Brahmabāndhav Upādhyāy* (Delhi: ISPCK, 2000), 211–55.

53. Tennent, *Building Christianity on Indian Foundations*, 228.

54. Lesslie Newbigin, *The Relevance of Trinitarian Doctrine for Today's Mission* (London: Edinburgh House Press for the World Council of Churches, Commission on World Mission and Evangelism, 1963), 33.

55. The most perceptive historical work in my opinion is Flett, *Witness of God*, see esp. 123–62. Flett attempts to relate the ecumenical history of missions with the work of Karl Barth to see the connection (and disconnection) between the ecumenical missionary thoughts surrounding *missio Dei* and Barth's trinitarian theology. For a good historical discussion from an American Lutheran viewpoint, see James Scherer, *Gospel, Church, and Kingdom: Comparative Studies in World Mission Theology* (Minneapolis: Augsburg, 1987).

national Missionary Council's (IMC) conference in 1952 in Willingen, Germany, that the concept appeared widely. Although the Willingen meeting of IMC did not use the term, it employed the concept and thus is considered the birthplace of *missio Dei*.[56] Nevertheless, as John Flett indicates in his in-depth study, the popularization of the term following the conference and the inclusion of trinitarian language in the conference statement were not connected and had different sources. Hartenstein does not connect *missio Dei* with trinitarian theology in advocating *missio Dei*.[57] The trinitarian proposal came from the American preparatory study report "Why Missions?" While Hartenstein and most missions advocates remained Christocentric in their theology and missionary motivation, the American report proposed a move away "from vigorous Christo-centricity to thoroughgoing trinitarianism."[58] Section 2 of the conference's statement on the missionary calling of the church opens with this sentence: "The missionary movement of which we are a part has its source in the Triune God himself."[59] The section closes with a powerful statement obligating Christians to be in Christ's mission: "There is no participation in Christ without participation in his mission."[60] The significance of these statements is realized in later discussion. The term "participation," in particular, becomes a key term for understanding how the church does missions only by participating in the *missio Dei*. From this meeting, the groundswell of *missio Dei* as advocated by Hartenstein and other German mission scholars developed, marking a new chapter in the theological consideration of Christian mission.

While its rise in the story of the IMC from 1952 may appear as if it was a mere historical incident, *missio Dei* evolved in the ecumenical setting in part as a response to the psychosocial demand

56. David J. Bosch, *Transforming Mission: Paradigm Shifts in Theology of Mission*, 20th anniv. ed. (Maryknoll, NY: Orbis Books, 2011), 399.
57. Flett, *Witness of God*, 133.
58. "Why Missions? Report of Commission I on the Biblical and Theological Basis of Missions," 1952, Paul Lehmann Collection, Special Collections (Princeton Theological Seminary Library, Box 41.2, Princeton, NJ), 6, quoted by Flett, *Witness of God*, 140.
59. International Missionary Council, *Missionary Obligation of the Church*, 2.
60. International Missionary Council, *Missionary Obligation of the Church*, 3.

for a firm theological foundation of the missionary enterprise at the time. The missionary crisis of the mid-twentieth century produced a thirst for a theological justification of missions. The introduction of *missio Dei* and the trinitarian foundation were the outcomes of the quest, as shown by David Bosch. The brilliance of Bosch's book *Transforming Mission*, which I consider the missiological book of the twentieth century, lies partly in its identification of the shifting—and the nature of the shifted—paradigms of the Christian mission. Bosch locates one of the most profound paradigm shifts of missions between "the end of the modern era" and the emerging postmodern "ecumenical missionary paradigm."[61] The emerging new era is so rich that he dares to name only "elements" of the new paradigm. Yet, his "elements" are the most comprehensive theological themes we have seen so far. Readers of Bosch's masterpiece cannot miss the centrality of *missio Dei* in the new era, spreading into and underlying all the elements he pursues. Bosch identifies the historical groundwork of the new theologically rich missionary paradigm in the missionary crisis of the mid-twentieth century, as clearly demonstrated in the IMC's Willingen conference of 1952. No work has influenced the missionary thinking of the late twentieth and early twenty-first centuries more than Bosch's *Transforming Mission*. Nothing infused the *missio Dei* concept into the missiological deliberation of the thinking public more than this book.

The missionary crisis of the era in general and the inner tension of the missionary enterprise in particular burst open, so to speak, at the Willingen meeting. Dissatisfaction with the status quo of missions and deep disagreement on missionary principles were clear, especially within the group that was dealing with the theological statement of the conference theme, "the Missionary Obligation of the Church." The group failed to produce the theme statement as intended, and a substitute statement was produced, which ironically became the most far-reaching document of the conference and was foundational for the development of the theology of mission in the ensuing period. This was a surprising outcome for those attending the meeting. Lesslie

---

61. Bosch, *Transforming Mission*, 357, 377.

Newbigin expresses this well: "This meeting was widely thought at the time to have failed in its major task. But subsequent history has shown that it was in fact one of the most significant in the series of world missionary conferences."[62] What seemed like a small and insignificant conference at the time turned out to be one of the most important missionary conferences.

The concept of *missio Dei* gained traction quickly in the Protestant conciliar circles. Missionary thinkers of the mid-twentieth century connected the Christian missionary enterprise with the redemptive and reconciliatory mission of the triune God. Two contesting approaches quickly became apparent. One was a world-centered understanding, provocatively propounded by the Euro-American groups in their study "The Missionary Structure of the Congregation."[63] The other, a more traditional view that gave a central place to the church in God's mission, was upheld by several leaders and thinkers, including Newbigin[64] and Georg Vicedom.[65]

The theorizing of mission in the *missio Dei*, and thus the theological groundwork of missions, began largely in Europe and chiefly in Germany. However, implications of the theology for the life and practice of the church were drawn in the United States. These came under the label "missional church," which was also the title of a pioneering book published by the Gospel and Our Culture Network.[66] By "missional church," its proponents meant that the church should be defined primarily as God's missionary agent, as one being sent into the world. Its organizing principle itself should be mission, and

62. Lesslie Newbigin, "Mission to Six Continents," in *The Ecumenical Advance: A History of the Ecumenical Movement*, ed. Harold Fey, 3rd ed. (Geneva: World Council of Churches, 1993), 2:178.

63. This was a study project of the Department on Studies in Evangelism of the WCC. The study's final report was published as *The Church for Others and the Church for the World: A Quest for Structures of Missionary Congregations* (Geneva: World Council of Churches, 1968).

64. See Newbigin, *Relevance of Trinitarian Doctrine for Today's Mission*; Newbigin, *The Open Secret: An Introduction to the Theology of Mission*, rev. ed. (Grand Rapids: Eerdmans, 1995), 19–65.

65. Georg F. Vicedom, *The Mission of God: An Introduction to a Theology of Mission* (St. Louis: Concordia, 1965).

66. Lois Barrett and Darrell L. Guder, *Missional Church: A Vision for the Sending of the Church in North America* (Grand Rapids: Eerdmans, 2009).

its basic character is to be missionary. Instead of living for itself and primarily serving its members, the church's chief mission should be engaging the world, near and far, with the gospel: "Mission is not just a program of the church. It defines the church as God's sent people. Either we are defined by mission, or we reduce the scope of the gospel and the mandate of the church. Thus our challenge today is to move from church with mission to missional church."[67]

Lesslie Newbigin was the link between *missio Dei* emerging in the ecumenical European setting of the World Council of Churches (WCC) and missional church developing from the American missiologists who worked out the theology for the missionary practice of the church. After retiring from his missionary career in India, Newbigin began a new chapter of engaging missions in the West. Today, many consider this later work to be more significant than his long years of missionary work in India and his service in the ecumenical movement. His significance in the West is perhaps a natural outcome of his great missionary experience in India; in some ways, he helped bring the West on par with the non-West. Newbigin's most lasting legacy is the missional church movement he inspired in the West. The group of American missiologists of the Newbigin school who responded to his call for missionary engagements in the West as a missionary gauntlet[68] led the missional church movement. We will say more about this in chapter 4. Ironically, the movement did not see itself as hinging on the modern missionary movement and insisted on the *missio Dei* as its foundation.

Missions in Trinitarian Theology and the Modern Missionary Movement: Aquinas and Ignatius

"The Five Chapters" of 1539, the first foundational document of the Society of Jesus (the Jesuits), states that members of the society were banded together "by the vow we make to carry out without subterfuge or excuse and at once (as far as in us lies) whatever His

67. Barrett and Guder, *Missional Church*, 6.
68. George R. Hunsberger, "The Newbigin Gauntlet: Developing a Domestic Missiology for North America," *Missiology: An International Review* 19, no. 4 (October 1991): 391–408.

Holiness may order pertaining to the progress of souls and the propagation of faith, whether he decides to send us among the Turks, or to the New World, or to the Lutherans, or any others whether infidels or faithful."[69] Thus, the society's purpose is the progress of souls and the propagation of faith that they carry out under the authority of the pope. This translates as "missions" in the special "fourth vow" of the Jesuits, which reads in part, "I further promise a special obedience to the sovereign pontiff in regard to the missions according to the same apostolic letters and the Constitutions."[70] By adding this fourth vow to the three common vows of poverty, chastity, and obedience, the Jesuits make missions their special and distinct identity. In his study of the fourth vow, Jesuit historian John O'Malley shows the connection between "The Five Chapters" and the vow by stating that "two obligations of the vow emerge: (1) to go wherever sent by the popes, (2) to do whatever they order that pertains to the progress of souls and propagation of faith."[71] With the Jesuits and their fourth vow came the modern missionary movement in which "missions" came to mean being sent by the authority of the church to save souls and propagate the Christian faith.

Paul Kollman has helpfully traced the historical use of "mission" by Ignatius Loyola, the founder of the Society of Jesus, which he relates to the rise of missiology in the nineteenth and twentieth centuries.[72] Though Ignatius's use of the term was novel, Kollman points out that Ignatius seems to have employed the term "mission" casually,

69. Antonio de Aldama, "The Five Chapters," in *The Constitutions of the Society of Jesus: The Formula of the Institute, Notes for a Commentary*, trans. Ignacio Echaniz (St. Louis: The Institute of Jesuit Sources, 1990), chap. 2, https://jesuitportal .bc.edu/research/documents/1539_fivechapters/. "The Five Chapters" was originally approved by Pope Paul III in 1539, and a revision in 1540 was approved in the papal bull *Regimini militantis Ecclesiae*.

70. "The Formula of the Vows," in *The Constitutions of the Society of Jesus*, 527, quoted by John O'Malley, "The Fourth Vow in Its Ignatian Context: A Historical Study," *Studies in the Spirituality of the Jesuits* 15, no. 1 (January 1983): 1.

71. O'Malley, "Fourth Vow," 2.

72. Paul Kollman, "At the Origins of Mission and Missiology: A Study in the Dynamics of Religious Language," *Journal of the American Academy of Religion* 79, no. 2 (June 2011): 425–58. Kollman relates the use of "mission" in Ignatius and the Jesuits from the fifteenth century with the development of missiology in the nineteenth century.

without any formal explanation. Even in his interpretation of John 20:21, where the Vulgate uses the term, Ignatius shows no special use except for a literal interpretation to urge the society to do Christ's work in obedience to God's will.[73] Kollman further points out that the term (*missão* in Portuguese and *misión* in Spanish) was also commonly used in the colonial administrative setting for political and military outposts. While early Jesuit use was not formal or univocal, as time went on, the term increasingly came to mean "evangelization abroad."[74]

In recounting the spirituality of Ignatius with respect to missions, Catherine Mooney shows that Ignatius's pilgrimage to Jerusalem after his conversion "to outdo them [the saints] in penances" was also the beginning of his shift toward missions. Mooney says, "For Ignatius, mission trumps asceticism" as "apostolic mission gradually became the touchstone for Ignatius's choices."[75] Although the term "mission" is used here to interpret Ignatius's early career, it was to "help souls" or, more generally, to "help others" that defined the heart of his spiritual direction and thus his mission. In 1534, when Ignatius and his first six companions decided to go to Jerusalem, the decision was made so that they could "spend their lives there helping souls."[76] It was five years later, when the company had grown to ten, that the Jesuits expanded "The Five Chapters," declaring their submission to the pope to send them wherever he pleased, "pertaining to the progress of souls and the propagation of the faith."[77] "Missions," as the fourth vow calls it, thus involves being sent by the pope wherever he decides for the progress of souls and the propagation of the faith.

However, the word "mission" was not new in the Latin-speaking Roman Christianity of the West. Since Augustine of Hippo in the fifth century, the term had been employed in connection with what we now call the economic Trinity. Almost three centuries before Ignatius,

73. Kollman, "At the Origins of Mission," 430.
74. Kollman, "At the Origins of Mission," 432.
75. Catherine M. Mooney, "Ignatian Spirituality, A Spirituality for Mission," *Mission Studies: Journal of the International Association for Mission Studies* 26 (2009): 195.
76. Mooney, "Ignatian Spirituality," 196.
77. Mooney, "Ignatian Spirituality," 197.

Catholic theologian Thomas Aquinas had thoroughly elaborated the theological meaning of trinitarian mission in his magnum opus, *Summa Theologica*. Ironically, the two uses of the same term in the Roman Catholic Church, those of Aquinas and Ignatius, have not been related. Their existence in two different spheres (theology and missiology) seems to have separated them from each other. We turn to Aquinas's use of the term to show how it may theologically illumine the emergent modern missionary enterprise.

While much can be said about Aquinas's theology of the divine mission, a brief comment on question 43 of part 1 of the *Summa Theologica*, entitled "The Missions of the Divine Persons," will suffice to show the use and meaning of the term "mission" in trinitarian theology. The basic definition of the term as used is "send," yet its use in the trinitarian sense has much more meaning and significance. The term most significantly refers to the relationships among the divine persons in the Trinity. Gilles Emery writes, "The enquiry into the missions brings the study of the [divine] persons' mutual relations to a head: to think about the missions is still to consider the persons in their relationships, their divine being and their own properties."[78]

Question 43 is divided into eight articles that Aquinas considers individually and sequentially.[79] In articles 1 and 2, Aquinas deals with the meaning of "mission" by answering whether a divine person can be properly sent. The act of sending, he says, "implies a certain kind of procession of the one sent from the sender." Such a procession can either be "according to command, as the master sends the servant; or according to counsel, as an adviser [is being sent by] the king to battle; or according to origin, as a tree sends forth its flower."[80] The divine procession of the Son and the Holy Spirit, Aquinas argues, is a procession of origin from the sender as a flower is sent forth by a tree. In this sense, the one sent is not inferior to the sender. This is an important point for Aquinas as a rebuttal to the idea of divine subordination in the Trinity.

78. Emery, *Trinitarian Theology of St. Thomas Aquinas*, 362.
79. Unless otherwise stated, the translation of *The Summa Theologica* used throughout is Thomas Aquinas, *The Summa Theologica*, trans. Fathers of the English Dominican Province, http://www.documentacatholicaomnia.eu/03d/1225-1274 ,_Thomas_Aquinas,_Summa_Theologiae_%5B1%5D,_EN.pdf.
80. Aquinas, *Summa Theologica* I, q. 43, a. 1.

Refuting the idea that the one sent, by definition, is separated from the sender and "that whoever is sent, departs from one place and comes anew into another," Aquinas says that "the divine person sent neither begins to exist where he did not previously exist, nor ceases to exist where He was. Hence, such a mission takes place without a separation, having only distinction of origin."[81] In spelling out the divine mission through the Son and the Holy Spirit, Aquinas maintains the unity and equality of the divine persons in the one God. Later in article 4, Aquinas defends the reasonability of the sending of the Second and Third Persons of the Trinity and not the Father. Quoting Augustine's words that "the Father alone is never described as being sent," Aquinas states, "The very idea of mission means procession from another, and in God it means procession according to origin. . . . Hence, as the Father is not from another, in no way is it fitting for Him to be sent; but this [procession from another] can only belong to the Son and to the Holy Ghost, to whom it belongs to be from another."[82]

On "whether mission is eternal, or only temporal,"[83] Aquinas resolves that the divine mission is both eternal and temporal. "The procession," he says, "may be called a twin procession, eternal and temporal." The procession as God is eternal, and in his mission as the incarnated man, it is temporal. Furthermore, the mission is both visible and invisible.

The identification of *missio Dei* as the theological foundation of mission prompts us to relate Aquinas's theology of mission in the Trinity with the use of "mission" and its cognates to describe what we now call the missionary endeavor, as begun by Ignatius. Although I have not come across any work that relates these two, the potential theological fruit is great. Aquinas's concept of mission in the trinitarian context lends important insights into the ongoing theological explorations of the meaning of mission. We can only scratch the surface here.

In juxtaposing the two "missions," the most obvious difference is their authorizing sources. Papal authorization was strongly emphasized in the Jesuits' missions. However, a close reading of Igna-

81. Aquinas, *Summa Theologica* I, q. 43, a. 1.
82. Aquinas, *Summa Theologica* I, q. 43. a. 4.
83. Aquinas, *Summa Theologica* I, q. 43, a. 2.

tius's work clearly shows God to be the spiritual source of missions. In his study of Ignatian missions, Indian Jesuit scholar Michael Amaladoss relates the trinitarian roots of mission in Ignatian spirituality. "For Ignatius," he said, "his experience of God was a variety of relationships—distinct, though united and in a certain way articulated. We see an experience of unity—the sphere, the essence, the Trinity—an experience also of diversity as relationships to different Persons and an experience of order with the Father as the source and Jesus as the mediator."[84] Aquinas deals with God's mission of saving the world through the sacrificial mission of the Son as empowered by the Spirit. Consequently, the use of the term "send" as carefully crafted by Aquinas does not convey a hierarchy of relation but one of mutuality. The emphasis on the relationship among the divine persons is especially significant.

While God's work of salvation is undoubtedly presupposed, "missions" in the fourth vow of the Jesuit is blunt in its submission to the authority of the pope. Of course, as we see in the later history of the Jesuits, the society became a rival to the pope's authority, leading to its suppression at one point by papal authority. The ecclesiastical context of the Protestant Reformation and Catholic Counter-Reformation may have influenced the emphasis on papal authority. The intentional recognition of papal authority could have been intended to resist the Protestant challenge to the pope's authority. In the light of the twentieth-century theology of the *missio Dei*, the difference is on God as the source of the mission versus the church as the authorizing source of missions. In theory, the two sources should not collide, and the sovereignty of God should be maintained, but in practice, the church's authority has tended to overshadow God as the source of missions. The church's mission to propagate the good news of salvation is founded on God's mission in the world.

Missio Dei *in the Triune God's Economy of Salvation*

As the works of Rahner and others show, Aquinas has been criticized for separating the immanent Trinity and the economic Trinity.

84. Michael Amaladoss, *Mission Today: Reflections from an Ignatian Perspective* (Rome: Centrum Ignatianum Spiritualitatis, 1989), 29–41.

Much of this criticism originated in the trinitarian theology of the twentieth century, which has expanded the discussion significantly across different Christian traditions. Reactions against the Western trinitarian theology of Augustine and Aquinas were due in part to its heavy reliance on the Platonic philosophy of abstraction, which led to an emphasis on the immanent Trinity. The trinitarian revival today foregrounds the economic Trinity by recognizing the immediacy of epistemology. It does not negate the immanent Trinity nor obliterate ontology in the process. But practicality and realism largely trump abstractions and metaphysics, which are relatable only through speculation.

Aquinas's theology of the divine mission shows that the goal of trinitarian mission in the world is the economy of salvation. In the procession of the Son and the Holy Spirit, or in the sending of the Second and Third Persons of the Trinity, God brings salvation to the world. Insofar as faith in Jesus as the Christ or Jesus as God's revelation is the entry point into the trinitarian faith, the mission of sending Jesus into the world is the mission of God for the world. God's work in and for the world in the person of Jesus and in the power of the Holy Spirit for the world's salvation is God's world mission. The New Testament testimony of God's mission in Jesus may thus be generalized under two rubrics: (1) that which Jesus did in the world as a testimony to God and his reign, and (2) what his coming and going, which climaxed in the cross and the resurrection, mean for the world in God's providence. We will examine the economy of salvation as God's mission more fully in the next two chapters.

We may summarize the aspects of the development of trinitarian theology in relation to God's mission that we have discussed as follows:

- The epistemic limitation posed by scientific rationalism of the Enlightenment tradition suppressed the doctrine of the Trinity in the West for a few centuries. The doctrine was revived in the twentieth century, a revival we are currently experiencing.
- The recovery of the doctrine has an ecumenical platform, drawing its resources from both East and West. This development also highlights contributions of Christians in the Global South who took an active part in the revival. The renascent trinitarian

theology has been closely related to the theology of mission rooted in the *missio Dei* concept.

- The theological reconceptualization of Christian missions after the crisis of missions and the transition from modern to postmodern missions introduced *missio Dei* as a foundational concept. The revival of trinitarian theology and the emergence of *missio Dei* significantly impacted contemporary theology. This led us to review the use of "mission" in Aquinas's trinitarian discussion and in Ignatius's modern missionary work in order to establish a theological source of missions.

- By foregrounding the economic Trinity, the ongoing renaissance of the doctrine of the Trinity highlights the divine mission in the world, and thus, the *missio Dei*. Reflection on Aquinas's theological work on the divine mission has the potential to serve the missionary enterprise.

- The revived trinitarian theology and mission as *missio Dei* intersect and mutually inform each other in the economy of salvation.

The Incarnation and the Mission of God

It is reasonable to begin a discussion on the Trinity with the doctrine of the incarnation because the doctrine of the Trinity is conditioned on faith in the divinity of Jesus as the Christ. The doctrine was formalized as the church affirmed Jesus Christ as God, together with the Holy Spirit. However, in tracing the mission of God, we begin with the triune God and describe the incarnation as his mission in the world. This helps our effort to identify a theology of mission within the larger body of theology. The incarnation, or God becoming human, is the means God has chosen to accomplish his mission of saving the world. As indicated previously, the economic Trinity as a way of expressing God's self-revelation and his identification with human history provides a pathway for understanding God's mission in the world. Because the doctrine of the incarnation is key to understanding the economy of the trinitarian mission, we briefly deal with the topic here as the principal channel of the *missio Dei*. At the same time, we will draw out the implications for understanding a theology of culture later.

The Incarnation as the Means of God's Mission

The Latin term *incarnatio*, from which derives the English "incarnation," literally means that "the Word or Son of God was 'made flesh' or 'in-carnated' by assuming a complete human nature and not simply an external bodily form."[85] The incarnation, as "the first aspect of the work of Christ,"[86] is the way in which the mission of God's salvation of the world is accomplished in and through Jesus Christ. So deep and far reaching is the doctrine that Gerald O'Collins exclaims, "Our questions and conclusions should never pretend to master the truth of the incarnation."[87] Prompted by the teaching of Arius that Jesus was "like" God the Father and not "of the same essence," the church took up the discussion of Jesus's divine identity, together with the idea of incarnation. It took more than a century to settle on the divinity of Jesus Christ, and the division between Chalcedonian and non-Chalcedonian continues even to this day.

The rich history of the church's dealings with incarnation-related doctrines and themes, including the divinity of Christ (Christology) and the triunity of God, is key to understanding the topic of incarnation. When the Council of Nicaea in AD 325 affirmed Jesus as "God from God, light from light, true God from true God, begotten not made, consubstantial (*homoousion*) with the Father, through whom all things came into being . . . ,"[88] the verdict against Arianism seemed clear. However, the issue was far from settled, and the church took several more decades to clarify and restate the Nicene Creed in the Council of Constantinople (AD 381).[89] A related question concerning the relationship between Jesus's divinity and humanity emerged in the first quarter of the fifth century due to a controversy attributed to Nestorius. The church debated the divine-human nature of Jesus at the Council of Chalcedon (AD 451), which settled the matter—while

85. Gerald O'Collins, *Incarnation*, New Century Theology (London: Continuum, 2002), 1.

86. Oliver Crisp, introduction to part 3 of *A Reader in Contemporary Philosophical Theology*, ed. Oliver Crisp (London: T&T Clark, 2009), 145.

87. O'Collins, *Incarnation*, vii.

88. Critical edition of the creed from Giuseppe L. Dossetti, *Il Simbolo di Nicea e di Costantinopolis* (Rome: Herder, 1967), 226–41, quoted by Anatolios, *Retrieving Nicaea*, 18.

89. See Anatolios, *Retrieving Nicaea*, 19–28.

acknowledging the inherent mystery—by affirming Jesus to be fully human and fully divine. Yet some theologians still question whether this conclusion is satisfactory. Some continue to voice dissatisfaction with the council's use of Greek metaphysics in its formulation of the doctrine.[90] We will return to the creed or "definition" of the Council of Chalcedon later.

Three books of the New Testament—the Gospel of John, Paul's Letter to the Philippians, and the Letter to the Hebrews—highlight the incarnation of Christ in different ways.[91] John proclaims that the "word" (*logos*) God spoke at creation through which all things were made, the word spoken through the law at Mount Sinai and the prophets in history, God's word with which God is identified—that word of God has become flesh in the person of Jesus and dwelled among us (John 1:1–14). Although the word (*logos*) John discusses best suits God's "word" as used in Judaism, the meaning was often melded with other philosophical thought of the time, such as Stoicism and Platonism. That was what the contemporary Jewish writer Philo did in his discussion of *logos*. In early Stoicism, the term often refers to "the rational principle of the universe," and Philo used it as "a way of speaking about the creative plan of God that governs the world."[92] Even if John had these other sources in mind, they do not contradict but supplement the Jewish theology of the word, which seems central for John.

If John's expression has an aura of majesty and power, the expression in the Letter to the Hebrews (1:1–3), though quite similar in content, appears relatively casual. If John presumes a knowledge of the power and majesty of the word, the author of Hebrews aims to show that Jesus, the Son of God, is "the reflection of God's glory and the exact imprint of God's very being" (1:3). Recalling what God had done in Jewish history and contrasting those acts with what he

---

90. Alister E. McGrath, "Incarnation in the Western Tradition," in *The Cambridge Dictionary of Christianity*, ed. Daniel Patte (Cambridge: Cambridge University Press, 2010), 589.

91. Here I am following Gerald O'Collins in the selection of these texts from John, Paul, and the Letter to the Hebrews. See O'Collins, *Incarnation*, 2–4.

92. E.g., Philo, *On Creation* 17–24. See Gail R. O'Day, "The Gospel of John: Introduction, Commentary, and Reflections," in *The New Interpreter's Bible*, ed. Leander E. Keck (Nashville: Abingdon, 1995), 9:519.

is doing "in these last days . . . for us through the Son," Hebrews expresses the finality of God's word spoken through the incarnated Son.

While John and the author of Hebrews present the dramatic event of the incarnation, Paul in Philippians 2:5–11 uses hymnic language to express the self-emptying "mind of Christ" in the incarnation. He describes the "emptying" of Jesus's divine eternal being for his human body "in the form of a slave," as well as his death, resurrection, and ascension. Paul aims to show the incredible self-humbling commitment of Jesus, who refused to exploit his equality and existence in the form of God and instead emptied himself as a slave to become like us even to the point of death, like a sinner. While John and the author of Hebrews discuss the uniqueness of Christ's incarnation as the one and only event of God becoming human, Paul invites Christians to model the incarnating mind of Christ for themselves. Whereas the Gospels, especially Matthew and Luke, place the virgin's conception of Jesus as the key to understanding the incarnation, Paul emphasizes the accomplishment of the incarnation by relating it with the entirety of Christ's work for the salvation of the world.

Belief in the divinity of Jesus defines Christianity. Any compromise on this—Jesus as the divine-human savior of the world—betrays the Christian faith. In their comparative study of the incarnation in Judaism and Christianity, Jacob Neusner and Bruce Chilton reduce the concept of the incarnation to the manifestation of God in human history.[93] According to Neusner, if something in Judaism can be compared to Jesus's role as God's manifestation in Christianity, then it is the Torah. While Neusner and Chilton's concepts of the incarnation may not be far off from the point, their treatment defies an essential aspect of the doctrine—namely, the particularity of the Christian doctrine. By interpreting the incarnation as they do, the two scholars generalize what is characteristically unique: God becoming a particular human being in a particular time and space. Jews and Christians do indeed part ways on the identity of Jesus, and the incarnation is a key dividing concept.

Placed in the larger context of world religions, the doctrine of the incarnation appears unreasonable, especially for its particularity.

93. Jacob Neusner and Bruce D. Chilton, *God in the World*, Christianity and Judaism—The Formative Categories (Harrisburg: Trinity Press International, 1997).

From his missionary experience among Hindus in India, Lesslie Newbigin describes how scandalous the particularity of the incarnation and salvation of Jesus Christ sound to Hindus: "To a devout Hindu, heir to four thousand years of profound religious and philosophical experience, there is something truly scandalous in the suggestion that to put it crudely, he or she must import the necessities for salvation from abroad. 'Is it really credible,' the Hindu will ask, 'that the Supreme Being whom I and my ancestors have loved and worshipped for forty centuries is incapable of meeting my soul's need, and that I must await the coming of an agent of another tradition from Europe or North America if I am to receive his salvation?'"[94] Such objections have prompted some Christian scholars to explain away the doctrine. John Hick treats it as a mere metaphor: "My thesis concerning the Christian doctrine of incarnation is that as a literal hypothesis it has not been found to have any acceptable meaning. . . . But on the other hand, as religious metaphor or myth the idea of incarnation communicates something of momentous importance about Jesus, something that forms the basis of distinctively Christian experience and faith."[95] Yet against such mythologizing and limiting of the doctrine to metaphorical category, Niels Hendrik Gregersen claims that "today, the pendulum has swung in favor of speaking of [i.e., affirming] God's incarnation and embodiment."[96]

A few of the questions raised against the incarnation may help to exemplify its intricacies. How exactly do the two natures of Christ unite? Some argue for a perichoretic relationship, analogous to the explanation of relationships in the Trinity. The term *perichoresis* as used by the church fathers expresses the depth of intimacy in the relationship of the two natures of Christ (or the three persons in the Trinity), such that they become one.[97] Let's consider another question. Does

94. Newbigin, *Open Secret*, 66.
95. John Hick, *The Metaphor of God Incarnate: Christology in a Pluralistic Age*, 2nd ed. (Louisville: Westminster John Knox, 2005), 106.
96. Niels Hendrik Gregersen, introduction to *Incarnation: On the Scope and Depth of Christology*, ed. Niels Hendrik Gregersen (Minneapolis: Fortress, 2015), 2.
97. The term as used may be translated as "co-indwelling" or "interpenetrating" between the two (natures of Christ) or three (beings in the godhead). For the christological use of the term, see Oliver D. Crisp, *Divinity and Humanity: The Incarnation Reconsidered* (Cambridge: Cambridge University Press, 2007), 1–2.

the enfleshment of the Son of God limit his divine omnipotence and omnipresence? Or how does the incarnate Christ maintain his divine omnipresence as God? This question has been discussed under the technical rubric of *extra Calvinisticum*, according to which "the eternal Son of God, during his incarnate life on earth, was not enclosed by or limited to the physical body of Jesus Christ but continued to uphold the universe by virtue of maintaining a form of presence beyond or outside Jesus' physical body."[98] The expression *extra Calvinisticum* has been coined in opposition to the Lutheran position, in which the incarnate Jesus is omnipresent since the two natures cannot be divided.

So foundational is the doctrine of incarnation that its theological implications continue to multiply, even as its historical explanations continue to be questioned and reinterpreted. Many of the discussions on Christology, soteriology, and the Trinity are connected to and integrated in incarnation theology. In the next chapter, we will look into the economy of God's salvation. Most of the classic theologies of salvation are done in connection with the question of incarnation. Irenaeus's theology of salvation is a response to the question "*Ut quid enim descendebat?*" (For what purpose did Christ come down from heaven?),[99] and Athanasius outlined his soteriology in his book *On the Incarnation*.[100] Similarly, Anselm's famous satisfaction theory of atonement responds to the question in the title of his book *Cur Deus homo?* (Why God became man).[101]

Gerald O'Collins's helpful book *Incarnation* shows how specific incarnational themes are combined with general Christology, soteriology, and trinitarian topics. After laying out the meaning of incarnation, O'Collins discusses themes of Christology—including Christ's divine and human natures, one divine person in two natures, and the incarnation and salvation[102]—together with other related questions.

98. James R. Gordon, *The Holy One in Our Midst: An Essay on the Flesh of Christ* (Minneapolis: Fortress, 2016), 1.

99. Quoted in Gustaf Aulén, *Christus Victor: An Historical Study of the Three Main Types of the Idea of Atonement*, trans. A. G. Hebert (Austin: Wise Path Books, 2016), chap. 2, Kindle.

100. Athanasius of Alexandria, *On the Incarnation*, trans. Penelope Lawson (n.p.: Blue Letter Bible, 2012), Kindle.

101. Anselm, *Cur Deus homo?* (Why God became man) (London: Religious Tract Society, 1900).

102. O'Collins, *Incarnation*, chaps. 6, 7, 8, and 10.

The richness of the doctrine has also been demonstrated through the variety of its theological and spiritual implications. Following Paul's challenge to have the mind of Christ at the incarnation, missiologists and practical theologians have dealt with the implications of incarnation for ministry and mission under such themes as incarnational mission and ministry. "Deep incarnation," a theme that has recently surfaced, treats the incarnation of Christ as "a radical embodiment that reaches into the roots of materials and biological existence." Driven by this theme and challenged by the question "Is God incarnate in all that is?" a group of scholars recently produced a book "on the relationship between the incarnation in Christ and wider concerns of a theology of creation."[103] Amid such ongoing investigations on the meaning and implications of the incarnation, our concern is the incarnation's implications for God's missionary work in the diverse cultures and societies of the world. As the channel of God's mission in the world, what significance does the incarnation have?

In Time and Space—God of History, God in History

"To do Christology is to inscribe Christ into the times and cultures we inhabit," Graham Ward rightly states.[104] In his presidential lecture to the Society for the Study of Theology delivered at St. Edmund's Hall, Oxford, in March 1968, T. F. Torrance dealt with the topic of incarnation in relation to space and time. We devote this section to discuss Torrance's lecture in order to draw out some implications for the gospel-culture relations that will be dealt with later in the book. Torrance begins by describing what he calls "an utterly staggering doctrine":

> By the Incarnation Christian Theology means that at a definite point in space and time the Son of God became man, born at Bethlehem of Mary, a virgin espoused to a man called Joseph, a Jew of the tribe and lineage of David, and toward the end of the reign of Herod the Great in Judea. . . . Thus it is the faith and understanding of the Christian Church that in Jesus Christ God Himself in His own Being has come

103. Gregersen, *Incarnation*, 1–2.
104. Graham Ward, *Christ and Culture*, Challenges in Contemporary Theology (Oxford: Blackwell, 2005), 2.

into our world and is actively present as personal Agent within our physical and historical existence.[105]

The doctrine does not mean, he continues, that God has become "wholly into what He was not." Instead, it means "that the Son of God has become man without ceasing to be the God He ever was, and that after the Incarnation He is at work within space and time in a way He never was before."[106] Here, we may recall Aquinas on the procession of the Son from the Father. The divine processions of the Son and the Holy Spirit from the Father, Aquinas insists, is a procession of origin like a flower coming from a tree. There is no separation between the flower and the tree. What are the temporal and spatial significance of the incarnation, and what does the divine identification with creaturely human beings mean? To connect the theology of incarnation with space and time, Torrance identifies the principal conceptions of space and time in the history of Western thought as "the receptacle notion" and the "relational notion." Although the receptacle notion, drawn from Greek thought, was rejected by the early church fathers, it came to occupy an important place in Western thought.[107]

Torrance then outlines four ways we can think of the incarnation in relation to space and time. One's view defines how one comes to understand God-world relations. The first way in which theologians relate the incarnation to space and time is to understand it as the entry of the Son of God into a finite receptacle. This is the approach taken by Thomas Aquinas and Martin Luther. Aquinas avoids the limiting aspect by insisting that Jesus became human without leaving his divine throne. Luther uses a kenotic explanation of Christ's self-emptying to explain how Christ came to the finite, limiting container. However, Torrance maintains that Christ was not limited as a fully divine being even in his incarnate body. The second view is that of Isaac Newton, who asserts that God is the infinite receptacle and contains himself. Torrance dismisses both of these views, noting that the church fathers

105. Thomas F. Torrance, *Space, Time and Incarnation* (Oxford: Oxford University Press, 1969), 52.

106. Torrance, *Space, Time and Incarnation*, 53.

107. Torrance, *Space, Time and Incarnation*, 56–58.

also rejected the notion of a receptacle (though, as we will see, dismissing the first option entirely may not be most helpful).

The third view Torrance describes is that of Origen, advocated by E. A. Milne in modern times, according to which space, time, and all the orderly existence in and of the universe are the results of God's creative, active, and all-embracing power. God endowed the creation with his rationality. To Origen, this means "that God has limited Himself in the limitation of creation through its subjection to His own self-comprehension."[108] God is revealed through creation, and much of human rationalization about God is to be traced back to God. The potential problems with this position are in its limitation of God to the creation and in humanity's inability to explain futility seen in the world. Origen does differentiate between God's mind and the human mind, and he prioritizes God above even the "eternal intelligence" of creation.

The fourth view, which Torrance seems to choose, clearly distinguishes God's eternal rationality from created rationality in space and time. As the creator and sustainer of the universe, God is free from any necessity in the relationship with his creation. "Hence the Incarnation of the Son of God in the realm of space and time means that He assumes created truth and rationality and makes them His own although He is distinct from them."[109] An aspect of this has been debated under *extra Calvinisiticum*, as discussed above. Torrance identifies patristic theology, Anselm, Karl Barth, and others as offering different forms of this position. The danger of this position in its extreme form is that it tends to posit God as inscrutable.

In his further comments on the last view, Torrance makes two points of interest for us. The first is a distinction he makes between how God can relate with the world and how the world can relate with God. He says, "We must think of God's relation to the world in terms of an infinite differential, but we must think of the world's relation to God in terms of a created necessity in which its contingence is not negated." In other words, the relationship is not neutral, and the very capacity of the relationship is different. Whereas "God is free from any necessity" in his relationship to the world, the world's

108. Torrance, *Space, Time and Incarnation*, 64.
109. Torrance, *Space, Time and Incarnation*, 65.

relation to God is bound within "the concepts and laws that arise within space and time."[110] Torrance's second point of interest is the centrality of the incarnation in the relationship between God and the world. It is the only way that has been made available to human beings to relate to God. The incarnation is "the decisive action of God in Christ which invalidates all other possibilities and makes all other conceivable roads within space and time to God actually unthinkable." The relationship between God and human beings, therefore, is possible only through Jesus Christ. He (Jesus Christ) is *the place* in all space and time where God meets with man in the actualities of his human existence, and man meets with God and knows Him in His own divine Being."[111] The incarnation in the God-human being of Jesus Christ is the only way known to us where the triune God's mission of saving the world occurs.

We need not limit the ways of relating the incarnation with human history under Torrance's four views, yet what he provides illustrates the manners and possibilities. Following his choice of a relational notion over a receptacle notion, we can largely classify the options into two. The first, represented by Origen, closely relates God with the world and cultures to the extent that it also somewhat limits him to the world's affairs. Nature, cultures, and social affairs of the world are taken seriously in this view, as they are seen positively as God's handiwork. Sin and the fallen nature of the world are not emphasized. The second view, advocated in different forms by scholars including Anselm in the Middle Ages and Karl Barth in modern times, emphasizes God's sovereignty in relation to the world. Consequently, the incarnate Christ is distinguished from the world of space and time into which he was incarnated. To Anselm, says Torrance, "God is ineffably transcendent over all our conceiving of Him, yet our conceiving, when true, arises under the compulsion of the divine Being."[112] Torrance seems to prefer Anselm as a moderate thinker to Barth, as the former related theology with natural science much more closely. Torrance's differentiation between God's relation to the world and the world's relation to God is a helpful tool to understand this position's point.

110. Torrance, *Space, Time and Incarnation*, 67.

111. Torrance, *Space, Time and Incarnation*, 75 (emphasis original).

112. Torrance, *Space, Time and Incarnation*, 65.

2

GOD'S MISSION OF SALVATION (1)

*Biblical Images and Christological
Motifs of Salvation*

New Testament scholar Joel Green defines the term "salvation" in its biblical use as "the comprehensive term for all the benefits that are graciously bestowed on humans by God."[1] Understood in this broad and positive sense, the very religiosity of human beings has salvific significance. Yet more popularly, "salvation" has been used negatively to mean "deliverance from sin, death, and divine wrath."[2] While the more positive description tends to be general and has the capacity for a comprehensive understanding, salvation expressed in the negative mode tends to be focused, and its references are more specific. Thus, it has its own strengths and helpfulness. In recent ecumenical conversations, some Eastern Orthodox theologians have identified the positive sense of understanding salvation with Eastern and Oriental Orthodox churches. In contrasting the Western

---

1. Joel B. Green, *Salvation*, Understanding Biblical Themes (St. Louis: Chalice, 2003), 9.
2. Bruce Demarest, *The Cross and Salvation: The Doctrine of Salvation* (Wheaton: Crossway Books, 1997), 27.

conception of salvation as redemption with the Eastern Orthodox Church's conception of salvation as deification (or *theosis*), Vladimir Lossky says the sin-focused redemptive salvation shows "the negative aspect of the ultimate goal," whereas "deification," which considers "the ultimate vocation of the created beings," is a "positive definition of the same mystery."[3]

For our purpose, we will have both dimensions in mind, understanding salvation broadly as the divine blessing represented by various biblical images and metaphors in relation to different human situations and conditions. Salvation is founded in the overflowing love of God for the world, which has the power to impact every aspect of human life. One obvious biblical source for understanding salvation as God's blessing is God's covenantal blessing to Abraham (Gen. 12:1–3), which may be appropriately connected to the Hebrew concept of shalom as salvific wholeness. Christopher Wright persuasively argues that what Paul describes in Galatians 3 as the gospel of justification announced "beforehand to Abraham" (3:8) is God's covenantal promise to bless all nations through Abraham (Gen. 12:3).[4] To belong to Christ and affirm him as the savior is to be "Abraham's offspring, heirs according to the promise" (Gal. 3:29).

With their teachings on the meaning and purpose of existence, all religions offer salvation of some kind in their own ways. A religion's understanding and perception of God or the equivalent ultimate reality largely determine its conception of salvation. The Abrahamic faith family of Judaism, Christianity, and Islam sees God as personal, holy, and morally perfect in contrast to imperfect humanity. Thus, salvation and sin are closely related. But for religions such as Brahmanic Hinduism that view God in nonpersonal terms, salvation or its nearest equivalents do not necessarily relate to sin but to finding the right way or path. Whether in the Buddhists' four noble truths and eightfold path, the Islamic Shahadah (that there is no God but Allah, and Muhammad is his prophet), or the Hindu dharma (both in personal *svadharma* and eternal *sanatana dharma*), there is a promise

---

3. Vladimir Lossky, *In the Image and Likeness of God*, ed. John H. Erickson and Thomas E. Bird (New York: St. Vladimir's Seminary Press, 1974), 110.

4. Christopher J. H. Wright, *The Mission of God: Unlocking the Bible's Grand Narrative* (Downers Grove, IL: IVP Academic, 2006), 194 (see 191–221).

of some kind of salvation as broadly defined. For religions that understand God to be morally demanding, religious legalism can be the consequence. The different images of salvation in Christianity, we will show later, can also be related to different aspects of the rich biblical images of God.

The present discussion identifies salvation as the core component—the basic message and the raison d'être—of Christian missions. There is a mission because there is salvation. God's salvific blessing is central to the triune God's mission in the world. In theological terms, what we call "mission" is about what God has done and is doing to eternally bless humanity and the entire creation by calling them to joyfully live the new life he imparted through his Son and to faithfully witness to that eternal salvific blessing. By being with and in him, we enjoy his gift of life, and by participating in what he is doing in the world, we become his missionaries. This mission, we claim, is the center of the entire theological gravity of Christianity. Thus, soteriology, or the study of salvation, is at the heart of the theology of mission.

Two early attempts to define missiology in the 1970s converge at salvation. One attempt looks at it objectively as God's saving work coming from above, and the other provides a view from below, as the subjective human experience of being saved. The first definition is by Dutch theologian-missiologist Johannes Verkuyl, who writes, "Missiology is the study of the salvation activities of Father, Son, and Holy Spirit throughout the world geared toward bringing the kingdom of God into existence."[5] Here the emphasis is on God's activities—what he has done and is doing, as well as the purpose behind his activities. It identifies salvation as what God has been doing in mission for the sake of his kingdom in the world. The second definition is by Australian anthropologist-missiologist Allan Tippett, who defines missiology as "the study of man being brought to God in history."[6] This statement places emphasis on the human side. Tippett expands his understanding of missions as "(1) the processes by which

5. Johannes Verkuyl, *Contemporary Missiology: An Introduction* (1978; repr., Grand Rapids: Eerdmans, 1987), 5.
6. Allan R. Tippett, "Missiology, A New Discipline," in *The Means of World Evangelization: Missiological Education at Fuller School of World Mission*, ed. Alvin Martin (Pasadena, CA: William Carey Library, 1974), 26.

the Christian message is communicated, (2) the encounters brought about by its proclamation to non-Christians, and (3) the planting of the Church and organization of congregation."[7] Since Tippett is an anthropologist, it is not surprising that he sees missiology as centering on the human side of the meeting with God. This view presupposes God's work of salvation and focuses on how it affects human beings.

In some ways, the two approaches together reflect the God-human identity of Jesus as the core of the salvation he brought. While it is impossible to separate the two sides (God's work and human reception of salvation), they show the two essential characteristics of missiology as an enterprise—namely, God's saving work and the human experience of transformational conversion. Since the focus of the present project is on God's work of salvation, our emphasis is on the former. If we were to explore the human side of the equation as Tippet has done, we would focus on the topic of conversion. Yet the boundary between salvation as God's gift of life and conversion as human reception of life is too fluid to be clearly demarcated, especially among the new Christians of the majority world.

Ghanaian feminist theologian Mercy Amba Oduyoye once declared, "The Christ in the popular theology of Africa is above all the one who saves."[8] Salvation in Jesus Christ is what attracts Africans to Christianity and makes it meaningful to them.[9] In a similar vein, Asian theologian Simon Chan observes that the ontological question about Christ's divine and human natures is not the priority for Asians: "Rather, the question of who Christ is usually surfaces in relation to what he does. The ontological status of Christ is presupposed, but the question in the foreground is his work as Savior."[10] At the heart of Latin American liberation theology is salvation as God's liberation to be lived out in our sociopolitical realities. Gustavo Guttiérez says, "To speak about a theology of liberation is to seek an answer to the . . . question: what relation is there between salvation

7. Tippett, "Missiology," 26–27.
8. Mercy Amba Oduyoye, *Beads and Strands: Reflections of an African Woman on Christianity in Africa* (Maryknoll, NY: Orbis Books, 2004), 18.
9. Oduyoye, *Beads and Strands*, 19.
10. Simon Chan, *Grassroots Asian Theology: Thinking the Faith from the Ground Up* (Downers Grove, IL: IVP Academic, 2014), 91.

and the historical process of human liberation?"[11] A response to this question, he adds, "presupposes an attempt to define what is meant by salvation, a concept central to the Christian mystery."[12] Whether in its spiritually confined understanding or in a relatively progressive humanistic understanding, salvation has been at the core of theology in the majority world. Not only did the relatively new Christians of Africa, Asia, and the Americas receive the message of salvation from the missionaries, they have been reimagining what it means to be redeemed in their revolutionary worlds. Salvation became so foundational in the emerging theology of the majority world after the missionary movement that a soteriological approach underlies most—if not all—their theologies. Whereas salvation has been imagined mostly as a methodical and juridical atonement in the West, theologians of the majority world have a wide range of soteriological references. Salvation conceptions range from supernaturally inclined spiritual mediation[13] to a transformative reconstruction of societies;[14] from profound salvific identification with the humanity and suffering of people[15] to revolutionary deliverance from oppression and bondage.[16] Because our focus is on God's work of salvation, we can only hint at these rich resources on the human experience.

11. Gustavo Guttiérez, *A Theology of Liberation*, trans. Candad Inda and John Eagleson, 15th anniv. ed. (Maryknoll, NY: Orbis Books, 1988), 29.

12. Guttiérez, *Theology of Liberation*, 83.

13. See, for instance, Kwabena Asamoah Gyadhu, "Mediating Power and Salvation: Pentecostalism and Religious Mediation in an African Context," *The Journal of World Christianity* 5, no. 1 (2012): 43–61.

14. For older reconstructionist soteriology in Africa, see the works of Jesse Mugambi and Charles Villa-Vicencio, etc. For newer works calling for the transformation of imagination, see the works of Kä Mana, Emmanuel Katongole, and others. For a discussion on this theme, see David T. Ngong, *The Holy Spirit and Salvation in African Christian Theology: Imagining a More Hopeful Future for Africa* (New York: Peter Lang, 2010), 47–69.

15. Asian theologians have expressed God's identification with the sufferings of people in various ways. Kazoh Kitamori's *Theology of the Pain of God* is an example. In *The Compassionate God*, C. S. Song highlighted Jesus's death, entry into the "womb of darkness," and suffering messiahship as his way of salvation. See C. S. Song, *The Compassionate God* (Maryknoll, NY: Orbis Books, 1982), 87–126.

16. In Asia, see the works of scholars such as C. S. Song and M. M. Thomas. Song situates salvation in the Asian revolutionary context and states, "Redemption is God's revolution." Song, "From Israel to Asia: A Theological Leap," *The Ecumenical Review* 28, no. 3 (July 1976): 254–55. Thomas uses "humanization" as the goal of salvation. See *Salvation and Humanisation* (Madras, India: The Christian Literature Society, 1971).

Jesus Christ and His Saving Work

On the theological concept of salvation, there are a few pressing questions to be clarified. The most immediate question is how we name what we are studying. Like every other theological matter, that which we have so far called "salvation" is a mystery. It is a mystery in that we can neither fully describe it nor speak about it directly. As Avery Dulles says, "Mysteries are realities of which we cannot speak directly. If we wish to talk about them at all we must draw on analogies afforded by our experience of the world."[17] Most "theological realities," including salvation, can only be explained analogously. The Bible uses a host of terms for what we call salvation, and Christians have interpreted these terms in a variety of ways over the past two millennia. All of the biblical terms represent different aspects of one divine matter. Do we have a comprehensive term for this divine matter that conceptually encompasses all these terms and aspects? In the Western English-speaking context, the term "atonement" may be more common, especially in academia, and "redemption" is also similarly popular. I would argue that "salvation" is the most popular and comprehensive nomenclature in the global context as an encompassing term for what we are discussing.

In its development in Christian tradition, "salvation" tends toward an inclusive and comprehensive meaning, although the comprehensiveness depends on use and interpretation. We can make similar cases for other terms, such as "redemption"[18] and "atonement,"[19] especially

17. Avery Cardinal Dulles, *Models of the Church*, exp. ed. (New York: Doubleday, 2002), 2.

18. For instance, *The Oxford Companion to Christian Thought* has "redemption" as its main substantive entry on the subject. But the entry describes redemption as a "metaphor for describing the saving work of Jesus." Under its entry on "salvation," it says, "Salvation shares the same basic meaning as redemption, [under which entry] it is discussed at greater length. Nevertheless, salvation is too important a word to be omitted, and has, moreover, a wider connotation." See Adrian Hastings, Alistair Mason, and Hugh Pyper, eds., *The Oxford Companion to Christian Thought* (Oxford: Oxford University Press, 2000), 598, 639.

19. The English term "atonement," coined by William Tyndale to translate the Latin *reconciliatio*, is derived from "at one" or "at onement" and has the potential to be interpreted broadly to include reconciliation (Alister E. McGrath, *Christian Theology: An Introduction*, 2nd ed. [Hoboken, NJ: Blackwell, 1997], 566). But its use to translate Hebrew *kaphar*, "to cover" or "to wipe off," made it quite specific

the latter, which is currently enjoying a renewed interest.[20] Yet their contemporary use tends to be limited to the Judeo-Christian context and Western Christianity.[21] No aspect of their meanings is outside what "salvation" could contain. John McIntyre identifies at least thirteen biblical and theological "models of soteriology," including salvation. However, not only does he use "soteriology," which is derived from the Greek *sōtēria* (salvation), as the encompassing name, but his definition of salvation as a model is most comprehensive. He says that the model of salvation "pervades not only almost all the biblical talk about the death of Christ, and God's purpose revealed therein, but gathers up the whole of God's will for his people as we are given to understand it throughout the entire history of the people of Israel."[22] Our choice of the word "salvation" is based mainly on its cross-religious and interdisciplinary character.[23] In its broad sense, we employ it as a prevalent concept that encompasses all aspects represented by varying images of God's salvific work for the world and humanity.

Most christological studies throughout Christian history have dealt with the question of how Christ accomplished the salvation of the world. Related to this broader question are two other important issues for the present study. The first involves the person and work of Christ, which is often distinguished in Christology. How does salvation as the work of Christ relate to the person of Christ? That is, what has Christology to do with soteriology? Can the two be done independently? The second question, closely related, involves the role

---

in its sacrificial references and in taking a "more restricted meaning" (C. L. Mitton, "Atonement," in *The Interpreter's Dictionary of the Bible*, ed. Keith R. Krim and George A. Buttrick [Nashville: Abingdon, 1962], 1:309).

20. This "wholly and indigenously English" term "atonement" has gained increasing popularity since the turn of the twenty-first century. Paul Eddy and James Beilby, "The Atonement: An Introduction," in *The Nature of the Atonement: Four Views*, ed. James Beilby and Paul R. Eddy (Downers Grove, IL: InterVarsity, 2006), 9.

21. We should note that the meaning of "atonement" has been significantly expanded in Christian theological circles. See, e.g., Adam Johnson, "Atonement: The State and Shape of the Doctrine" and various other chapters in the *T&T Clark Companion to Atonement*, ed. Adam J. Johnson (London: Bloomsbury, 2017), 1–17.

22. John McIntyre, *The Shape of Soteriology: Studies in the Doctrine of the Death of Christ* (Edinburgh: T&T Clark, 1992), 33.

23. McGrath, *Christian Theology: An Introduction*, 386–87.

of Christ's death and resurrection in his work for salvation. Did Jesus accomplish the work of salvation only in his death and resurrection? Does his earthly ministry play a salvific role as well?

While distinguishing the "person" and the "work" of Christ can be helpful, the two cannot be separated. When it comes to Jesus Christ, there is also the matter of faith. Faith in his identity as divine and human is linked to his work, and the meaning and significance of his work are also faith driven and are understood in the light of his identity. Therefore, the two are intrinsically related: there is no Christology without soteriology, and there is no soteriology without Christology. As much as his work of salvation makes Jesus the savior, his being the God-man is his salvific call and, thus, his saviorhood. Yet for the sake of clarity, his person and work may be dealt with separately without losing sight of their integrity. Perhaps, the two elements may be essentially understood as two entry points into one entity. We can argue that Paul and the authors of the Synoptic Gospels employ these two different entry points to write about Jesus Christ. Writing before the Synoptic Gospels were completed, Paul treats the goal of Christ's incarnation as accomplished in his death and resurrection.[24] He treats the coming and going of Christ as a single event through which God's salvation is worked out. He rarely refers to the life and teaching of Jesus and does not reference any stories about Jesus except the Lord's Supper and some apocalyptic images.[25] The responsibility to account for the life and teaching of Jesus fell to the authors of the Gospels, especially Mark, Matthew, and Luke. Each carefully collected the stories of Jesus's life and ministry, which scholars believe were circulating in many individual forms (pericopes),[26] and integrated them meaningfully into whole stories.[27] Their books became the foundation for understanding who Jesus is and how he achieves the salvation of the world.

24. Robert Wall appropriately calls this "vertical Christology." See Robert W. Wall, "Introduction to Epistolary Literature," in *The New Interpreter's Bible*, ed. Leander E. Keck (Nashville: Abingdon, 2002), 10:376.

25. Wall, "Introduction to Epistolary Literature," 10:376.

26. As the method of form criticism suggests; see, e.g., Christopher M. Tuckett, "Jesus and the Gospels," in *The New Interpreter's Bible*, ed. Leander E. Keck (Nashville: Abingdon, 1994), 8:77–81.

27. On redaction criticism, see Tuckett, "Jesus and the Gospels," in *The New Interpreter's Bible*, ed. Leander E. Keck, 8:83–85.

From a Christian canonical viewpoint, therefore, it is crucial to integrate the life story, ministry, and teaching of Jesus (from the Gospels) with the salvific meaning of the Christ event (from Paul). But such integration is not always easy to maintain, and a weakness of many studies is an imbalance in dealing with these two parts: the person of Christ and his salvific work. There are scholars, especially among so-called evangelicals, who emphasize Christ's work of salvation in his death and resurrection at the expense of consideration for his life and ministry. The entire person of Christ is often confined to a narrow understanding of salvation. On the other hand, numerous academic studies on the person of Christ lack any substantive treatment of his salvific work. Furthermore, obsession with the historical-critical method has led many scholars of the Gospels to disregard the obvious climax of the Gospels' accounts: the death and resurrection of Christ. An important challenge in our day is to treat the story of Jesus Christ in a holistic manner.

Does salvation, then, relate only to his death and resurrection? What part of Jesus's life and what portion of his work were salvific? Drawing from the response of John Galvin to the question "Which aspect of the existence of Jesus Christ is viewed as salvific?" Catholic theologian Robin Ryan outlines four main salvific points of reference in Jesus Christ.[28] The first is the incarnation. According to Ryan, certain theologians in the early church who espouse the salvific significance of the incarnation see "that the becoming flesh/human of the Son of God was itself transformative of the human situation, and even of the entire cosmos."[29] The Nicene Creed clearly embraces this conception of salvation. The second salvific point of reference in Jesus is his "words and deeds" during his public ministry.[30] Through Jesus's healing, exorcism, teaching, and table fellowship, people "experienced God's saving presence in their lives."[31] Ryan notes that in recent times liberationist and feminist theologians have reemphasized this aspect of salvation that is often underplayed in Christian tradition.

28. Robin Ryan, *Jesus and Salvation: Soundings in the Christian Tradition and Contemporary Theology* (Collegeville, MN: Liturgical Press, 2015), xvii–xx.
29. Ryan, *Jesus and Salvation*, xviii.
30. Ryan, *Jesus and Salvation*, xviii, 25–29.
31. Ryan, *Jesus and Salvation*, xviii.

Third, of course, the death of Jesus has always been the most dominant point of salvific reference for Christians, beginning with Paul in the New Testament period and extending through all of Christian history. Jesus's death and resurrection are considered the culmination of his earthly ministry. For Christians, his death has never been simply a brute fact of history. He "died for our sins in accordance with the scriptures," as articulated by the earliest Christian tradition handed down to the apostle Paul (1 Cor. 15:3). In fact, the death of Jesus for the salvation of the world has been considered "integral to the revelation of God's intention for the world."[32] The fourth and last point of reference is the resurrection. Treated mostly in connection with Jesus's death, the raising of Jesus from death by God is fundamental to Christian belief and is the foundation for the Christian hope of resurrection, as testified by witnesses recorded in 1 Corinthians 15.

From the entire New Testament, and especially the Gospels and the Letters, a strong case can be made for the death, resurrection, and ascension of Christ as pivotal in his mission of salvation. "The life of Jesus is single-mindedly directed toward his self-offering [at the cross]," states Fleming Rutledge.[33] The presentations of Christ's passion in the four Gospels are clearly distinguishable from the rest of the Gospel narratives. Rutledge points out their special place: "The passion stories take up one-fourth to one-third of the total length of the four Gospels, and biblical interpreters generally agree that the material was shaped by the church's oral traditions prior to being put into written form, in a way that forever indicates the surpassing importance of the suffering of Christ for the life of the earliest Christian communities."[34] Nothing in the New Testament contradicts the idea that the death and resurrection of Jesus are the culmination of his salvific work: he completed his missional work through his death, resurrection, and ascension, where his life story climaxed.

But it is from this pivotal point that the salvific significance of the rest of his life and ministry are understood. Jesus was not just one of the miracle performers; the realization of the salvific meaning of his death and resurrection helped early Christians to understand the

32. Ryan, *Jesus and Salvation*, xix; see also 29–33.
33. Fleming Rutledge, *The Crucifixion* (Grand Rapids: Eerdmans, 2015), 31.
34. Rutledge, *Crucifixion*, 42.

soteriological significance of all his miracles and teachings. Once understood that way, the salvific meaning of Jesus's teaching and miracles is not secondary. In fact, his entire story from birth to death and resurrection came to be understood as one soteriological event. The integration of Jesus's identity, life, and work is such that each part of the narrative—his eternal being before creation, the incarnation, and his public ministry—has salvific significance.

While the references to different parts of Jesus's existence should not be understood in isolation, history has shown that Christians of different periods, confessional traditions, and social and cultural locations have found particular metaphors and interpretations to be more meaningful than others. In many cases, these metaphors point to a particular aspect of Jesus's existence (life, ministry, works, death, resurrection), and such aspects can serve as a point of entry into the entire realm of Christian faith. In dealing with what we term "salvation," Christian history shows the richness of the concept, which no single term or image can fully represent. It is also important to recognize that Christians have had multiple entry points into the understanding and experience of God's salvation in Christ.

Biblical Images and Historical Theories of Salvation

God's work in Jesus Christ in the Christian tradition is about the salvation of all creation. The Bible as a whole testifies to God's work of saving humanity together with the rest of creation. A dominant narrative in the Old Testament and a major point of reference for Israel as the covenant people is the story of God's saving them from bondage in Egypt. The extended story of liberation or deliverance (the exodus) from bondage is punctuated by instructions for the atonement of sins and by the laws for keeping the covenantal relationship with God. From Abraham to Moses and all the prophets, God's mission of saving the world illustrated in the saving of his people is clear. When it comes to the new covenant, the very name of the person through whom the new covenant is promulgated means "savior": Jesus (*yeshua* in Hebrew). As Gabriel instructed Joseph, "You are to name him Jesus, for he will save his people from their sins" (Matt. 1:21). The idea of salvation is not just in the name but in the very goal of his coming, as Jesus himself declared to Nicodemus: "For God so loved the world that he gave his only Son . . . in order that the world might be saved through him" (John 3:16–17). The entire New Testament hinges on the story of God's salvation in Jesus Christ. There is no question about the centrality of salvation in the Bible. The Bible portrays God's work as a mission to save.

As discussed in the previous chapter, the God behind this mission of salvation is characterized in the form of three persons (Father, Son, and Holy Spirit). It is through the Second Person that the salvation of this triune God has been worked out. Yet, all three are involved. No singular way of describing the process and meaning of this salvation exists. Christians of different periods and places have drawn the meanings and implications of salvation from their spiritual experiences in a variety of ways and have presented them using different images and metaphors. The Bible abounds with such testimonies. Terms and language to describe the meanings of this salvation are largely determined by time and space. While salvation itself is believed to be eternal, the words describing it are time bound. Yet such words continue as they are interpreted and reinterpreted with new and expanded meanings from age to age and generation to generation.

The Bible uses the language of the time to describe the saving works of God in Christ. Scholars have clustered biblical terms and images in different ways. Focusing on the saving effect of the death of Jesus Christ, and not so much on the experiential aspect, Joel Green and Mark Baker see "five constellations of images" in the New Testament, noting that each of them "is borrowed from the public life of the ancient Mediterranean world."[35] These images are "the court of law (e.g., justification), the world of commerce (e.g., redemption), personal relationship (e.g., reconciliation), worship (e.g., sacrifice) and the battleground (e.g., triumph over evil)."[36] While these images center on the death of Jesus, some are also evident in the ministry of Jesus. A different example is a study by Brenda Colijn, who restates New Testament metaphors and

35. Joel B. Green and Mark D. Baker, *Recovering the Scandal of the Cross: Atonement in New Testament and Contemporary Contexts* (Downers Grove, IL: InterVarsity, 2000), 23.
36. Green and Baker, *Recovering the Scandal*, 23.

images for salvation and interprets them for today's globalizing world. Combining God's work and the human experience of salvation, she lists a wide variety of salvific images in the Bible. The list includes the inheritance of the new covenant, citizenship of a new country (the kingdom of God), a fresh start, rescue, liberation, and others.[37]

Green and Baker show the diversity of salvific images resulting from Jesus's death in the New Testament. Writing from a postresurrection perspective, Paul places his main emphasis on the atoning significance of Christ's death and resurrection and uses a variety of images to show different aspects of salvation.[38] Green and Baker select two texts—namely, 2 Cor. 5:14–6:2 and Gal. 3:10–14—to demonstrate Paul's use of multiple images of salvation even within a short paragraph. For instance, beyond reconciliation as the most obvious in the former (2 Cor. 5:14–6:2), one can detect vicarious substitution, representation, sacrifice, justification (implicitly), forgiveness, and new creation.[39] Similarly, the latter (Gal. 3:10–14) also integrates various images in a meaningful way.[40]

The Synoptic Gospels highlight the unjust suffering, humiliation, and painful death of Jesus. The resurrection is very significant in their presentations of Jesus's triumph over sin and death,[41] but their attention is not on its meaning or implications. While the Gospel of John shows the crucifixion to be pivotal and presents it ironically as glorification or exaltation, Luke focuses instead on Jesus's "exaltation" in his resurrection and ascension as the means of salvation.[42] These differences in the portrayal of salvation and the use of multiple images do not present contradictory messages about salvation. Instead, they show the conceptual richness of salvation in the Bible as it is appropriated in different contexts.

In his observation of studies on salvation in New Testament books by a group of South African scholars, Jan G. van der Watt points out

---

37. Brenda B. Colijn, *Images of Salvation in the New Testament* (Downers Grove, IL: IVP Academic, 2010), 23.

38. Green and Baker, *Recovering the Scandal*, 46; Donald Senior, *Why the Cross?* (Nashville: Abingdon, 2014), 79.

39. Green and Baker, *Recovering the Scandal*, 58.

40. Green and Baker, *Recovering the Scandal*, 60.

41. Senior, *Why the Cross?*, 23–28.

42. Green and Baker, *Recovering the Scandal*, 77–79, 71–73.

the unity and diversity of the theology of salvation. The studies show a rich and powerful soteriology in the New Testament. The theological and linguistic diversity should be "seen as reflecting the integration of the message into particular situations of the people involved in the first and original communication process."[43] Scholars have recognized the diversity of metaphors for salvation and the unity in its meaning and significance for some time. Since the early decades of the twentieth century, New Testament scholars such as Vincent Taylor have recognized "variety rather than uniformity" as characteristic of the New Testament's presentation of Christ's salvation.[44] As Joel Green concludes, the Bible has "not one but many models of atonement," yet clearly with "some common threads."[45]

While controversies and debates led to the canonization of the New Testament books and the doctrines of Christ (Christology) and the Trinity, it has been different with the doctrine of salvation. "The Church has not saught to canonise any specific *theory* of the death of Christ," says John McIntyre.[46] Just as we see a variety of images in the different books of the New Testament, there has been diversity and flexibility in the doctrine of salvation that allowed multiple theories to develop. Different images of salvation reflecting different theological views have been emphasized at different times. For instance, the idea of God's triumph over the devil through the ransoming of his Son was a significant image for the church fathers, especially since Irenaeus. But such an image was not as significant in later Western studies. Reflecting the strong notion of divine justice, Anselm's rational and legalistic approach influenced Western theological concepts, including the justification theory championed by Martin Luther and the penal substitution theory. Enlightenment thinkers and liberals

---

43. Jan G. van der Watt, "Conclusion: Soteriology of the New Testament: Some Tentative Remarks," in *Salvation in the New Testament: Perspectives on Soteriology*, ed. Jan G. van der Watt (Leiden: Brill, 2005), 505.

44. Vincent Taylor, *The Atonement in New Testament Teaching* (London: Epworth, 1940), 11, quoted in Joel B. Green, "Theologies of the Atonement in the New Testament," in *T&T Clark Companion to Atonement*, ed. Adam J. Johnson (London: Bloomsbury T&T Clark, 2017), 115.

45. Green, "Theologies of the Atonement," 133, 134.

46. John McIntyre, *The Shape of Soteriology: Studies in the Doctrine of the Death of Christ* (Edinburgh: T&T Clark, 1992), 1 (emphasis original).

emphasized stimulating and motivating human goodness through love and grace, resulting in social harmony as a way of salvation.

No study on salvation or atonement in Christian theological circles would be complete without mentioning three traditional theories of atonement that dominated Western theological studies on the topic: ransom or Christ the victor theory, satisfaction theory, and moral exemplar theory. Together these theories formed the most dominant ideas on salvation in the Western church. In advocating *Christus Victor* as the "classic theory" of salvation against the other two theories, Gustaf Aulén, in the early 1930s, helped to establish the three as representative theories in the West. The first one, Christ the victor theory, is characterized as dramatic, satisfaction theory as "objective," and moral exemplar theory as "subjective." As Aulén has argued, Christ the victor theory is as equally objective in nature as satisfaction theory is.

Christ the Victor Theory

Some call it "ransom," and others, especially after Aulén's study, use "Christ the victor." It may sound strange to modern readers to have "ransom" and "victor" together as one theory, since a victor would not need to pay a ransom. But the combination did not sound strange to the early church fathers, especially to Gregory of Nyssa. Gregory taught that, like an unsuspecting fish swallowing bait on a fishhook, Christ triumphs over the demons and the devil to pay the ransom under the veil of his humanity.[47]

Aulén argues that Christ the victor theory was most dominant until the late medieval era when Anselm's objective satisfaction theory became popular and was then contested by Abelard's subjective exemplar theory. The two new theories then came to dominate in the Western church. Aulén sets out to recover what he calls the "classic" idea of atonement: "Its central theme is the idea of the Atonement as a Divine conflict and victory; Christ—Christus Victor—fights against and triumphs over evil powers of the world, the 'tyrants' under which mankind is in bondage and suffering, and in Him God reconciles the

47. Daniel L. Migliore, *Faith Seeking Understanding: An Introduction to Christian Theology*, 2nd ed. (Grand Rapids: Eerdmans, 2004), 182–83.

world to Himself."[48] Despite the fact that many modern theologians have been skeptical of this theory for contemporary soteriology, it has been revived in recent decades. The renewal may be connected to postmodern criticism of the highly rationalized penal substitution theory, which is based on the violent death of Jesus.[49] Some theologians continue to push against this renewal, arguing the theory is no match for the substitutionary theory.[50]

Satisfaction Theory

Most popular and influential for traditional Christians in the West, especially Catholics, is the satisfaction theory of Anselm of Canterbury. Some consider it the first properly thought-out theory of salvation. The argument laid out by Anselm is complex, but the overall idea can be summarized briefly. By sinning through disobedience to God, humanity dishonored God and lost its intended eternal blessedness from God. But God's purpose cannot be frustrated, and the situation could only be remedied if satisfaction was made for sin. This satisfaction could be made only by one who was both human and God. "But God cannot properly leave anything uncorrected in His Kingdom," writes Anselm. "Furthermore, to leave sin unpunished would be tantamount to treating the sinful and the sinless alike, which would be inconsistent with God's nature. And this inconsistency is injustice."[51] It is simply unconscionable for God not to punish sin. Otherwise, "either God is not just to his own nature; or God is powerless to do what ought to be done, which is a blasphemous supposition. The satisfaction ought to be in proportion to the sin."[52] For this reason,

---

48. Gustaf Aulén, *Christus Victor: An Historical Study of the Three Main Types of the Idea of Atonement*, trans. A. G. Herbert (Austin: Wise Path Books, 2016), "The 'Classic' Idea of the Atonement" in chap. 1, Kindle.

49. See Marianne Meye Thompson, "Christus Victor: The Salvation of God and the Cross of Christ," *Fuller Seminary Studio*, accessed May 7, 2020, https://fullerstudio .fuller.edu/christus-victor-the-salvation-of-god-and-the-cross-of-christ/.

50. See, for instance, Richard Mouw, "Why *Christus Victor* Is Not Enough," *Christianity Today*, May 2012, 28–31.

51. Anselm of Canterbury, *Cur Deus homo* 1.11–21; 2.4–20, quoted in McGrath, ed., *The Christian Theology Reader*, 3rd ed. (Malden, MA: Blackwell, 2007), 356.

52. Anselm, *Cur Deus homo* 1.11–21; 2.4–20, quoted in McGrath, *Christian Theology Reader*, 356.

God became a man. Thus, "satisfaction cannot be made unless there is someone who is able to pay to God for the sin of humanity. This payment must be something greater than all that is beside God. . . . So nobody can make this satisfaction except God. And nobody ought to make it except human beings themselves. . . . and if God only can, and only humanity ought to make this satisfaction, then it is necessary that someone must make it who is both God and a human being."[53] Anselm's theory has some significant limitations and problems. For example, one may ask what kind of forgiveness is this? If God must punish, is there forgiveness? Daniel Migliore observes, "It draws upon the juridical metaphors of the New Testament in a way that brings mercy and justice into collision."[54]

The influence of this theory may be traced in at least two ways: the theory as it is continued in the penal substitution model, which will be discussed later, and the theory's inspiration to draw on a broader juridical foundation. As Alister McGrath states, "In taking up Anselm's approach, later writers were able to place it on a more secure foundation by grounding it in the general principles of law."[55] A strict reading of the theory allows only penal substitution as a legitimate offspring of the theory, but models including "representation" (Christ as the representative of humanity) and "participation" (believers as participating in Christ's death and resurrection) draw from it as well.[56] Through these, the central idea of Anselm's theory continues to dominate much of conservative soteriology in the West.

Moral Exemplar Theory

In the early third century, Clement of Alexandria pointed out that the love of God shown in the incarnation of Christ and especially expressed in his death demands the demonstration of a comparable love for God from humanity. Along the same line, Peter Abelard made a case that the incarnation intends to evoke love for God in human beings: "The purpose and cause of the incarnation was that Christ

---

53. Anselm, *Cur Deus homo* 1.11–21; 2.4–20, quoted in McGrath, *Christian Theology Reader*, 357.
54. Migliore, *Faith Seeking Understanding*, 184.
55. McGrath, *Christian Theology: An Introduction*, 402.
56. McGrath, *Christian Theology: An Introduction*, 402–3.

might illuminate the world by his wisdom, and excite it to love of himself."[57] Thus, Abelard's name has been associated with the moral exemplar or moral influence theory. The general idea of this theory is that salvation comes about in our love for God, as influenced by the love of God expressed in the incarnated Jesus Christ. Abelard has been misrepresented, according to McGrath, as reducing "the meaning of the cross to a demonstration of the love of God." McGrath argues that Abelard's soteriology is much broader and includes Christ's death as a sacrifice for human sin.[58] Abelard's emphases on the subjective impact of Christ's death and the benefit of loving God are especially significant for balancing the overly objectivistic teaching of Anselm. It highlights the transforming power of God's unconditional love.[59] John Wesley, for instance, taught the importance of the subjective effect of Christ through which Christians can attain "both higher degrees of holiness and higher degrees of glory."[60]

The theory has been reinterpreted to fit a variety of what we might call human-centered theologies. Italian Socinians reinterpreted it along with Renaissance humanism, saying Jesus was a model of what God morally expects from human beings.[61] The theory in its modified form then became the darling of Enlightenment theologians. These theologians tended to discard the transcendental aspect of the theory and emphasize salvation in relation to its moral impact on human beings.[62] The Enlightenment theologians' suspicion about the transcendental nature of Christian soteriology reverberates in various forms today—some secularized and others relativistic.

These revisions by the Socinians, Enlightenment theologians, and later progressive liberal theologians were done largely in reaction to the soteriology of the Protestant Reformation and its emergent tradition. Against the Protestant *sola gratia* and *sola fide* concept of salvation, some of these theologians emphasized the human meritorious works for salvation. But from the perspective of the Protestant

57. Quoted in McGrath, *Christian Theology: An Introduction*, 407.
58. McGrath, *Christian Theology: An Introduction*, 407.
59. Migliore, *Faith Seeking Understanding*, 185.
60. Kenneth J. Collins, *The Scripture Way of Salvation: The Heart of John Wesley's Theology* (Nashville: Abingdon, 1997), 85–86.
61. Demarest, *Cross and Salvation*, 153.
62. McGrath, *Christian Theology: An Introduction*, 410–11.

theology of grace, one may ask what exactly this evolving exemplar theory of salvation says about salvation. Does the theory as developed say salvation is earned by human repentance? As important as it is to love God, is it a cause for salvation or is it a grateful response to God for his salvation? For those who believe salvation to be God's gracious gift and not something earned by human beings, the moral exemplar or influence theory as it evolved is untenable as a theory of salvation. One can be an exemplary recipient of or respondent to God's salvation, but one does not earn salvation by exemplary love.

A Contemporary Integrative Summation

These three traditional theories of salvation—Christ the victor, satisfaction, and moral exemplar—are key themes in the history of understanding the multifaceted nature of God's salvation in Christ. Even as their influence reverberates in confessional traditions, the growing multicultural and social consciousness in societies around the world has necessitated fresh interpretations. Several current studies transcend the competing spirit evident in the three theories, and there have been more signs of integrating and enlarging the themes to show the rich motifs of God's saving work. The recent book by Fleming Rutledge is a good example, especially in the Western context.[63] Focusing on the death of Christ and its proclamation in the church, Rutledge brings together biblical motifs of salvation meaningfully without sacrificing scholarly depth. From as difficult a metaphor as "blood sacrifice" to an old and less popular concept like "recapitulation," Rutledge reinterprets salvation themes, making them palatable to contemporary taste.[64] More than anything, her work enlivens biblical themes on salvation and shows the multidimensional and rich doctrine of salvation.

While denominations and confessional traditions with their own histories of soteriological confessions have been learning from each other, their distinct emphases continue. The significance of salvation

63. Rutledge, *Crucifixion*.
64. See part 2, on "the biblical motifs" for her substantive treatment of each theme. Rutledge, *Crucifixion*, 207–570.

in Christianity is such that most denominations and confessional traditions came into being or identify themselves with their particular understanding or conceptual salvific emphasis. The Eastern Orthodox Church's conception can be summarized largely under *theosis* (deification), the Coptic Orthodox Church under forgiveness as a result of the sacrificial blood of Christ,[65] and Catholics under a largely sacramental interpretation, while Protestants generally agree on relating God's grace and the human response of faith.[66]

In today's multiconfessional, globalized environment, we see mutual influences, integration, and enrichment among the traditions. But confessional differences caused by competing soteriological theories have also been entering the denominations and traditions. While those taking a moderate theological stance tend to emphasize both the person of Jesus Christ (his identity) and his works in connection with salvation, conservatives tend to see salvation almost wholly in connection with Jesus's death and resurrection. For most Protestant evangelical Christians who hold to penal substitution, drawn from Paul's Letters, the death and resurrection of Christ are the key for understanding salvation. They tend to interpret Jesus's entire life and ministry through that lens. For others who give equal emphasis to the Gospels, especially the Synoptic Gospels, Jesus's teaching and ministry have high salvific value too. Pentecostal-charismatic Christians emphasize God's dramatic spiritual works, including exorcism and miraculous healing.

One major point of difference in the last few centuries is the view of the human condition. Until the central teaching of the Enlightenment changed the view on human beings as morally autonomous, most Christian traditions considered the doctrine of sin, including original sin, important. But most modernist thinkers object to the idea of the human sinful condition, and so the nature and importance

65. See H. H. Pope Shenouda III, *Salvation in the Orthodox Concept*, 3rd ed. (n.p.: Coptic Orthodox Patriarchate, 2005).

66. For a brief but clear summary of the different soteriological emphases of the different Christian traditions and denominations (with the exception of Coptic Orthodox), see Daniel J. Treier, "The New Covenant and New Creation: Western Soteriologies and the Fullness of the Gospel," in *So Great a Salvation: Soteriology in the Majority World*, ed. Gene L. Green, Stephen T. Pardue, and K. K. Yeo (Grand Rapids: Eerdmans, 2017), 16–23.

of the doctrine of salvation has changed.[67] As N. T. Wright points out, the problem with modernist-progressives is that they "cannot deal with evil."[68] Instead, they gloss over sin and evil with the myth of human goodness. With a positive view of human nature and ability, progressive liberals associate salvation with the moral growth of humanity as endowed. With the rise of human rights issues, beginning in the mid-twentieth century especially, the emphasis on human goodness and rights has taken hold of progressive thought and moved the idea of salvation away from sin.

67. Alister E. McGrath, *Iustitia Dei: A History of the Christian Doctrine of Justification, From 1500 to the Present Day* (Cambridge: Cambridge University Press, 1986), 136–48.

68. N. T. Wright, *Surprised by Hope: Rethinking Heaven, the Resurrection, and the Mission of the Church* (New York: HarperCollins, 2008), 85.

3

GOD'S MISSION OF SALVATION (2)

Dimensions and Scope of Salvation

Theorizing God's Salvation in the Global Church's Context

In a thorough and meaningful study on contemporary soteriology, Peter Schmiechen reconsiders and outlines current atonement theories. Among the significant observations he makes is that soteriology is contextual in nature. In agreement with some of the things we discussed in the previous chapter, Schmiechen sees the richness of salvation theories in various images coming out of different witnesses of Jesus. He points out that the different theories that emerged over time are explanations and appropriations of Jesus's life, death, and resurrection.[1] What is most helpful for the present study is how Schmiechen integrates different soteriological theories. His book and the volume by Rutledge mentioned in the previous chapter are two significant sources of inspiration for this chapter. We will propose a comprehensive integration of the theories of salvation for the global

1. Peter Schmiechen, *Saving Power: Theories of Atonement and Forms of the Church* (Grand Rapids: Eerdmans, 2005), 1–7.

church today. While Schmiechen inspires the structure, Rutledge informs the contents of some of the theories.

While Rutledge's disinclination to "theories" and her preference for "biblical motifs" are understandable, I do not agree that all theories are "spun out of human mental capacity."[2] In agreement with Schmiechen's use of atonement theories as drawn from biblical images "to provide an internally coherent explanation of Jesus' life, death, and resurrection,"[3] I will use both "theory" and "motif" as I see appropriate. Rutledge makes thorough analytical interpretations of some eight "biblical motifs," which she classifies broadly under two categories. Schmiechen draws up ten theories across four categories. We follow the lead of Schmiechen's categorization. Three of his four categories have three theories each, while one category is a theory in itself.

- Christ Died for Us. This category has three theories: (1) Sacrifice, (2) Justification by Grace, and (3) Penal Substitution.
- Liberation from Sin, Death, and Demonic Powers. This theory is a category in itself.
- The Purposes of God. There are three theories under this category: (1) The Renewal of the Creation, (2) the Restoration of the Creation, and (3) Christ the Goal of Creation.
- Reconciliation. This category has three theories: (1) Christ the Way to the Knowledge of God, (2) Christ the Reconciler, and (3) the Wondrous Love of God.

The first group, "Christ Died for Us," is broadly summarized as "redemption" in which the three main aspects of Christ's redemptive work are brought together. Sacrifice is a broad theme with a long history in Judaism. Schmiechen helpfully explains that the New Testament fuses and reinterprets various Old Testament sacrificial practices. The themes of justification by grace and penal substitution are drawn mainly from Paul's use of forensic language and concepts that largely interpret Christ's redemptive work.

2. Fleming Rutledge, *The Crucifixion* (Grand Rapids: Eerdmans, 2015), 210.
3. Schmiechen, *Saving Power*, 5.

In the second category, Schmiechen singles out liberation and out-lines the various forms and protagonists of this theology. He groups some early church fathers whose teachings are known for theories of ransom and the victory of Christ with contemporary liberation theologians, which seems a bit far fetched. A better classification is undoubtedly possible.

The name of the third group, "The Purposes of God," is a bit odd and unclear, and this category is the least convincing as a group of theories. What distinctly qualifies these theories as the purposes of God? Do other theories fall outside God's purpose? The common word in all three theories under this category is "creation." The theoretical difference between "renewal" and "restoration" is difficult to fathom from the discussion. The cases of Athanasius and Anselm in connection with creation are neither strong nor clear.

Schmiechen's last category is "Reconciliation," and its salvation theories relate to Christ as the knowledge of God (chap. 8), wisdom and power (chap. 9), and a demonstration of God's love and the establishment of a community of love for the world's redemption (chap. 10).

In addition to the weaknesses we have already noted, let me add two more. First, one expects a book written in the twenty-first century to reflect current trends in world Christianity, including traditions such as Pentecostal-charismatic Christianity. Second, one weakness of the approach is the use of cases for all the theories. While some examples are helpful, not all of them are convincingly appropriate or persuasive. For instance, the use of Anselm as a case for the restoration of creation does not produce a convincing theory, and the attempt to disconnect him from penal substitution is at best distracting. Furthermore, the tendency to limit thinkers and leaders to one or two theories and use them as advocates of those theories does not do them justice. Each one combines images and theories of salvation. As discussed earlier, even in a short passage like 2 Corinthians 5:14–6:2, we can identify numerous images of salvation. Just as Paul did, most theologians and thinkers work with multiple theories.

What is most helpful in Schmiechen's book is its integration of the different theories in a comprehensive manner, and his outline informs my own. I structure my own thoughts for contemporary soteriology in a broader context that includes the non-Western world. Given the shifting demographics of worldwide Christianity and the consequential changes of contexts for theology, I mix traditional theories with some soteriological themes and emphases from other traditions and parts of the world. During the past few decades, the Christian world has realized that there are more Christians in the non-Western world than in the West. Christians who now make up the majority are mainly charismatic and Pentecostal. I try to incorporate the salvific ideas and emphases of these new Christians. Looking at the ways various Christian bodies and traditions today have come to express their understanding of God's salvation in Jesus Christ, I group the most dominant theories of salvation as follows:

1. God's triumphal deliverance from oppressions and sufferings
   a. Christ the victor
   b. Liberation from sin, death, and demonic powers
   c. Healing and deliverance
2. God's redemptive forgiveness
   a. Ransoming sacrifice
   b. Justification by grace
   c. Penal substitution
3. Union with God
   a. *Theosis* (deification)
   b. Reconciliation with God and with other creatures
   c. Oneness with God
4. Restoration of life
   a. New birth
   b. Restoration of creation (or ecological renewal)

In other words, I think the entire theology of salvation encompasses four main themes: redemption, liberation, reconciliation, and renewal of life. All these themes and the encapsulated theories are familiar to Christians and may only need brief explanations. My intention is not to provide any detailed discussion but to structure the themes and discussions in the most integrative way possible. I will try to be brief and avoid repeating what other scholars have said. Although included as one among others, the significance of sacrificial imagery and its theoretical underpinning of most theories should be recognized. In one way or another, directly or indirectly, the notion of sacrifice relates to all the theories in the four groups. Christ sacrificed himself for the redemption, liberation, reconciliation, and renewal of the life of humanity, the world, and all creation.

God's Triumphal Deliverance from Oppressions and Sufferings

The first category considers salvation as sharing the victory of Christ in the liberation from death and all evil forces. God's triumph over all oppression and all resistance to the blessed life makes victory possible for his creation. Those who are oppressed can see Jesus's victory over Satan in various ways, including his works of exorcism and healing and overcoming temptations. His victory culminated in his death and resurrection. For those who believe their pain and suffering are caused by sin under Satan, Christ's victory over Satan, the great oppressor, means everything. Jesus's healing miracles and those performed in his name by his disciples, past and present, are nothing short of salvation in real time. Christ's triumph is a triumph over oppression, the oppressive structures, and the oppressor for those who see sin in structural forms as caused by greed and oppressive structures. It is a liberation to be claimed here and now and into eternity. Therefore, this theoretical group includes (1) Christ the victor model, (2) a broad understanding of the theology of liberation in its many forms, and (3) salvation as healing and deliverance from the spirit of death and darkness.

This group of salvation theories is dominant today in less sophisticated societies of the majority world. As Simon Chan suggests, elitist Christians and grassroots Christians have different emphases even within these categories.[4] If sociopolitical liberation defines elitists' soteriology, spiritual deliverance and victory-liberation are what grassroots Christians are looking for. Healing as deliverance from demonic power or evil spirits is not foreign to people of primal

---

4. Simon Chan, *Grassroots Asian Theology: Thinking the Faith from the Ground Up* (Downers Grove, IL: IVP Academic, 2014), 94–117.

religious backgrounds in Africa and Asia. In an empirical study of the concept of salvation among African Independent Churches in Nigeria in the 1970s, Kenneth Enang found that the primary meaning of salvation is "deliverance." He quotes leaders of these churches as expressing their uniform understanding of salvation:

> "Salvation is deliverance from the power of evil principalities and the enclaves of human enemies."
> "Salvation is liberation of man from the powers of the demon."
> "[Salvation is] the deliverance from the traps of evil beings."
> "[Salvation is] deliverance from ill health and misfortunes (of life)."[5]

Salvation as sociopolitical liberation made great headway in Latin America in the 1970s. While this view of salvation was first propounded by Catholics, Protestant evangelicals have also advocated what they consider to be a biblically centered version.[6] Thus, while conservative Christians in the non-Western world today tend to associate salvation as deliverance from evil power to God's goodness, in close consonance with the *Christus Victor* theory, progressive thinkers have popularly been associating salvation with social and political liberation. The latter strongly emphasizes the deliverance of marginalized people here and now.[7] To Pentecostal-charismatic Christians in much of Asia, Africa, and Latin America, Christ's salvific work is to be claimed in the power of the Holy Spirit. For them, Pentecost is not over, and the Holy Spirit continues to work signs and wonders supernaturally, delivering people from their sins and daily struggles in life.[8] As Amos Yong points out, Pentecostal scholars have been at the

---

5. Kenneth Enang, *Salvation in a Nigerian Background: Its Concepts and Articulation in the Annang Independent Churches* (Berlin: Verlag von Reimer, 1979), quoted in John S. Mbiti, *Bible and Theology in African Christianity* (Nairobi: Oxford University Press, 1986), 152.

6. For a brief discussion on salvation in Latin America as advocated by Catholic scholars and Protestant evangelicals, see Lalsangkima Pachuau, *World Christianity: A Historical and Theological Introduction* (Nashville: Abingdon, 2018), 119–23.

7. Pachuau, *World Christianity*, 100–103.

8. J. Kwabena Asamoah-Gyadu, "Signs, Wonders, and Ministry: The Gospel in the Power of the Spirit," *Evangelical Review of Theology* 33, no. 1 (2009): 32–46.

forefront in recovering biblical "Spirit Soteriology," which includes deliverance, healing, and liberation of the poor and oppressed.[9]

Thus, this group of salvific theories combines a revised *Christus Victor* theory with the exodus motif. The experience of Christians in the majority world is a combination of charismatic supernaturalism and revolutionary liberation. Fleming Rutledge treats the two themes separately and substantially in the Western Christian context. She relates the theme of *Christus Victor* meaningfully with the revival of apocalyptic theology in the West during the last fifty years[10] and then reinterprets the biblical theme in that light. Apocalypticism, which relates to the expectation of Christ's triumphal second coming, is a prominent belief in much of the majority world's Christianity. Many first come to accept Jesus and Christianity as the triumphal deliverance from suppressive traditions to the gracious God, and they live by faith in the triumphant return of Christ.[11] What attracts Africans to Christianity, according to the Ghanaian feminist theologian Mercy Amba Oduyoye, are images of "the Warrior-Saviour of the Hebrew Scripture"[12] and the accompanying image of "the Liberator."[13] The victory of Christ is claimed in the power of the Holy Spirit through healings, exorcisms, and various forms of Spirit baptism. If liberation is a form of God's deliverance for liberation theologians, for Pentecostals deliverance is the ministry of exorcism through the manifestation of the Holy Spirit.

Salvation as God's Redemptive Forgiveness

At the heart of this second group is the broad understanding of salvation as sacrificial redemption, the working out of which is logically present in the justice of God. In this group, we include (1) ransoming

9. Amos Yong, *The Spirit Poured Out on All Flesh: Pentecostalism and the Possibility of Global Theology* (Grand Rapids: Baker Academic, 2005), 88–91.

10. Rutledge, *Crucifixion*, 348–60.

11. See Lalsangkima Pachuau, "Mizo 'Sakhua' in Transition: Change and Continuity from Primal Religion to Christianity," *Missiology: An International Review* 34, no. 1 (2006): 41–57.

12. Mercy Amba Oduyoye, *Beads and Stands: Reflections of an African Woman on Christianity in Africa* (Maryknoll, NY: Orbis Books, 2004), 19.

13. Oduyoye, *Beads and Stands*, 21.

sacrifice, (2) justification by grace, and (3) penal substitution. These have dominated the concept of salvation in the Western church, influencing much of the rest of the world. Ransoming sacrifice is perhaps the most prominent concept in the Bible with respect to salvation and has such broad implications that it is impossible to limit it to just one category. Drawn from sacrificial traditions of Judaism and their interpretations in the New Testament, sacrificial ransom theory has rich metaphorical meanings. Most other salvific metaphors in the Bible are either drawn from or related to sacrifice. The sacrificial language used in the New Testament is the foundational concept to describe the salvific works of Christ, including ransom for many, Paul's justification and reconciliation, and the entire eucharistic tradition. Built broadly on the sacrificial concept, justification by grace and penal substitution incorporate courtroom concepts and have much of their foundation in retributive justice. As mentioned before, Anselm's satisfaction theory paved the way for much of the forensic explanation for redemption, which eventually distinguished the soteriological tradition of the West from the Eastern Church's soteriology. Our argument here is that other dominant theories like justification and penal substitution continue the tradition established by Anselm in Western soteriological tradition. The most substantive and meaningful biblical-theological treatment for contemporary Christianity on this group of salvific themes is provided by Rutledge, and we can only point readers to her work for further engagement.[14] Our brief historical discussion below centers on how church traditions embrace and interpret the themes.

Gustaf Aulén attempted to separate Luther from Anselm, highlighting their differences.[15] However, despite these differences, when placed in the broader context of the discussion, the two seem to have more in common than Aulén would have us believe.[16] On their commonality, Burnell Eckhart concludes, "Both Luther and Anselm

---

14. See Rutledge, *Crucifixion*, chaps. 6, 7, 8, and 11.

15. Gustaf Aulén, *Christus Victor: An Historical Study of the Three Main Types of the Idea of Atonement*, trans. A. G. Hebert (Austin: Wise Path Books, 2016), Kindle, see "The Historical Perspective" in chap. 1.

16. For an excellent response to Aulén on this, see Ted Peters, "The Atonement in Anselm and Luther: Second Thoughts about Gustaf Aulén's *Christus Victor*," *Lutheran Quarterly* 24, no. 3 (August 1972): 301–14.

speak in terms of payment for sin, of substitution, and of redemption by the blood of Christ."[17] Further attempts to differentiate penal substitution theory from justification can appear superfluous. Similarly, penal substitution and Anselm's satisfaction theory share the same basic idea: payment of the debt owed to God through Christ's death. Green and Baker opine that the shift from Anselm's satisfaction theory to modern penal substitution theory is merely at the level of legal framework, a change from medieval "feudal obligation" to the modern "criminal-justice system."[18] The difference between justification by faith and penal substitution is even harder to see. Today, we tend to associate justification with Lutheran and penal substitution with traditional Reformed theology. While the two seem mutually dependent and may be described as different aspects of the same entity, not only do some Lutheran advocates distinguish them, but a few even refute the idea of substitution in the theory of justification.[19]

The doctrine of justification (righteousness) is often seen as the defining soteriology of the Protestant Reformation. Yet the Reformers were not necessarily in one accord. Martin Luther championed justification theory, and it became the foundation of the reformation of the church after him. The theme of "the righteousness of God" that once haunted him became the key to Luther's understanding of God's salvation. Late in his life, the year before he died, Luther reflected back on his struggle and how he made his theological breakthrough: "At last, God being merciful, as I meditated day and night on the connection of the words 'the righteousness of God is revealed in it, as it is written; the righteous shall live by faith,' I began to understand that 'righteousness of God' as that by which the righteous

17. Burnell F. Eckhart, *Anselm and Luther on the Atonement: Was It Necessary?* (San Francisco: Mellen Research University Press, 1992), 191.

18. Joel B. Green and Mark D. Baker, *Recovering the Scandal of the Cross: Atonement in New Testament and Contemporary Contexts* (Downers Grove, IL: InterVarsity, 2000), 142.

19. These points are highlighted in the debate between David Brondos and Karl Donfried on the former's radical interpretation of Paul's theology of the cross and rejection of the substitution idea in his book *Paul on the Cross: Reconstructing the Apostle's Story of Redemption*. See Karl P. Donfried, "Paul and the Revisionists: Did Luther Really Get It All Wrong?," *Dialog: A Journal of Theology* 46, no. 1 (Spring 2007): 31–40, esp. 35–36; David A. Brondos, "Paul, Luther, and the Cross: Dialog with Karl Donfried," *Dialog: A Journal of Theology* 46, no. 2 (Summer 2007): 174–76.

live by the gift of God, namely by faith, and this sentence, 'the righteousness of God is revealed,' to refer to a passive righteousness, by which the merciful God justifies us by faith."[20] Living according to God's gracious gift of justification by faith became the distinctive mark of Luther's theology. This new understanding, he declared, "made me feel as though I had just been born again."[21] Unlike Luther, early Reformed theologians such as Huldrych Zwingli and Martin Bucer were strongly moralistic in their theories of atonement and rarely highlighted justification as a theory of atonement.[22] It was John Calvin who kept the theme of justification alive in the Reformed circles and close to Luther's understanding. Alister McGrath carefully summarizes justification in the Lutheran and Reformed literature between 1530 and 1700 as follows:

1 Justification is defined as the forensic *declaration* that the believer is righteous, rather than the process by which he is made righteous, involving a change in his *status* rather than his *nature*.

2 A deliberate and systemic distinction is made between *justification* (the external act by which God declares the sinner to be righteous) and *sanctification* or *regeneration* (the internal process of renewal within man). Although the two are treated as inseparable, a notional distinction is thus drawn where none was conceded before.

3 Justifying righteousness, or the formal cause of justification, is defined as the alien righteousness of Christ, external to man and imputed to him, rather than a righteousness which is inherent to him, located within him, or which in any sense may be said to belong to him. God's judgement in justification is therefore *synthetic* rather than *analytic*, in that there is no righteousness within man which can be considered to

---

20. Martin Luther, "Preface to the Latin Works (1545)," in *D. Martin Luthers Werke: Kristisch Gesamtausgabe* (Weimar: Böhlau, 1938), 54:185.12–186.21, quoted in *The Christian Theology Reader*, ed. Alister E. McGrath, 3rd ed. (Malden, MA: Blackwell, 2007), 440.

21. Luther, "Preface to the Latin Works," 185.12–186.21, quoted in McGrath, *Christian Theology Reader*, 440.

22. Alister E. McGrath, *Iustitia Dei: A History of the Christian Doctrine of Justification, From 1500 to the Present Day* (Cambridge: Cambridge University Press, 1986), 32–35.

be the basis of the divine verdict of justification; the righteousness upon which such a judgement is necessarily based is external to man.[23]

Although Luther has been identified with justification theory and Calvin with "the first fully worked out account of penal substitution,"[24] both seem to have freely employed these two and other concepts in their soteriology. These theories are developed and refined over time. For instance, John Wesley and Karl Barth supplemented penal substitution theory with the holy love of God as the motivating factor of the atonement, while keeping the substitutionary core intact.[25] An example of a good reinterpretation of penal substitution is Barth's "The Judge Judged in Our Place."[26] In recent years, both justification and penal substitution have been challenged from different angles. Nevertheless, they have dominated much of the Protestant tradition, and conservative and evangelical orthodox Christians have strongly defended them.

Salvation as Union with God

In the history of Christian theology, the expression "union with God" has been used to mean more than one thing. Most popularly, it refers to the mystical experience of the soul's ascension as taught by various mystical theologians in history. Such theology has a long history: from Hellenistic Judaism to early church teachers and then to Macarius-Symeon (also called Pseudo-Macarius) in fourth-century Syria,[27] Dionysius the Areopagite (or Pseudo-Dionysius) after the fifth

23. McGrath, *Iustitia Dei*, 2 (emphasis original).
24. Stephen R. Holmes, "Penal Substitution," in *T&T Clark Companion to Atonement*, ed. Adam J. Johnson (London: Bloomsbury T&T Clark, 2017), 307.
25. On Wesley, see Kenneth J. Collins, *The Scripture Way of Salvation: The Heart of John Wesley's Theology* (Nashville: Abingdon, 1997), 80–86. On Barth, see Daniel L. Migliore, *Faith Seeking Understanding: An Introduction to Christian Theology*, 2nd ed. (Grand Rapids: Eerdmans, 2004), 184.
26. For a meaningful treatment, see Rutledge, *Crucifixion*, 507–23.
27. See Matthew Friedman, *Union with God in Christ: Early Christian and Wesleyan Spirituality as an Approach to Islamic Mysticism* (Eugene, OR: Pickwick, 2017). Friedman traces the mystical theology of union with God from Judaism to early Christianity and then to the theology of John Wesley, which he relates to the Islamic Sufi tradition.

century (whose mystical theology of union with God greatly influenced Albert the Great and Thomas Aquinas),[28] and Meister Eckhart in the fourteenth century.[29] Related to this line of development is the soteriological tradition of union with God called *theosis* (deification) in the Greek-speaking Eastern Orthodox Church. Within a broad understanding of "union with God" in salvific terms, we place (1) Paul's concept of reconciliation and its various implications together with (2) deification (*theosis*). But the salvific meanings and implications of union with God exceed these two themes as traditionally applied in the church's life. Thus, we also recognize (3) oneness with God.

As already noted, the English word "atonement" was first introduced by William Tyndale to translate the word "reconciliation." Although the term has acquired a much broader meaning today and has taken on both redemptive and forensic meanings, its meaning of "at-one-with God" is a basic translation of the biblical meaning of reconciliation. Reconciliation, according to Paul, is primarily with God and consequently with other human beings and creatures. Paul's use of the term "reconciliation" or "reconcile" in four key passages (Rom. 5:8–11; 2 Cor. 5:14–21; Col. 1:20–21; Eph. 2:12–17) shows that it is always God who initiates and effects reconciliation; it is mentioned never as a process but always as a completed act.[30] Two of these passages (Rom. 5:8–11 and 2 Cor. 5:14–21) refer to God's reconciliation as it affects God and human beings directly; the last two include references to reconciliation in the entire creation and between human beings. As will be seen in the next section, being at-one-with God should necessarily lead to being at-one-with other creatures and fellow human beings. As presented by Paul, reconciliation is also

28. See Bernhard Blankenhorn, *The Mystery of Union with God: Dionysian Mysticism in Albert the Great and Thomas Aquinas* (Washington, DC: The Catholic University of America Press, 2015).

29. See Richard Kieckhefer, "Meister Eckhart's Conception of Union with God," *Harvard Theological Review* 71, nos. 3–4 (July–October 1978): 203–25.

30. E. C. Blackman, "Reconciliation, Reconcile," in *The Interpreter's Dictionary of the Bible: An Illustrated Encyclopedia in Four Volumes*, ed. Keith R. Crim and George A. Buttrick (Nashville: Abingdon, 1962), 4:17.

God's vocation for human beings.[31] Yet, focusing on the human task of reconciliation to the neglect of reconciliation with God runs the risk of turning the theme into mere rhetoric. In a theological consideration of reconciliation at a research institute at King's College, London, in 1999, a group of scholars reiterated the importance of the vertical Godward reconciliation before drawing the horizontal sociocultural and political dimensions of the theme.[32] Reconciliation among human beings cannot be divorced theologically from reconciliation with God. The need for conciliatory existence among people of different cultures, nationalities, religions, races, and ethnicities is even greater in today's globalizing world. The ideas of Christ as the reconciler between humanity and God (2 Cor. 5:18–21) and among people groups (such as Jews and gentiles in Eph. 2:14–20) are intrinsically related.[33]

The words of Irenaeus on deification (*theosis*), rephrased and repeated by Athanasius, Gregory of Nazianzus, and Gregory of Nyssa, that "God made himself man, that man might become God"[34] have become a well-known theological refrain. If reconciliation is a familiar concept in connection with God's uniting work with and among human beings, until recently deification has been used almost exclusively by Eastern Orthodox Christians in connection with God's cosmic salvation. Together with the revival of patristic theology in the nineteenth and twentieth centuries, the concept of deification has enjoyed new prominence in the Eastern Church. In today's globalized context, the concept has been recovered, broadened, and popularized even outside the Orthodox Church.[35] Whereas the traditional

31. Philip G. Ziegler, "A Brief Theology of Reconciliation," *Touchstone*, October 2016, 7–13.

32. The point is seen in the introductory summary of the papers by Colin Gunton. See Colin E. Gunton, introduction to *The Theology of Reconciliation*, ed. Colin E. Gunton (London: T&T Clark, 2003), 1–11.

33. See Lalsangkima Pachuau, "Ethnic Identity and the Gospel of Reconciliation," *Mission Studies* 26 (2009): 49–63.

34. Vladimir Lossky, "Redemption and Deification," in *In the Image and Likeness of God*, trans. John H. Erickson and Thomas E. Bird (New York: St. Vladimir's Seminary Press, 1974), 97.

35. A new interpretation of Luther's theology of justification by the Mannermaa school at the University of Helsinki claims *theosis* in Luther and seeks to interpret justification, among other things, as participation in God and *theosis*. See Veli-Matti

interpretation in the Eastern Orthodox Church seems to have re-stricted the understanding of deification to "become god by grace, or become 'a partaker in the divine nature' . . . (II Peter 1:4),"[36] recent interpreters expand the reference to describe other changes salvation works in human beings with respect to God, including "imitation of God," "in-dwelt by God," and "being re-formed by God."[37] As Alister McGrath says, "A distinction must be drawn between the idea of deification as 'becoming God' (*theōsis*) and as 'becoming like God' (*homoiosis theoi*)."[38] The former is associated with the Alexandrian school and the latter with the Antiochene school.

At the heart of this salvific concept is God's work of love to draw all creatures to himself. Defending deification as part of God's re-demptive work for the entire creation, Andrew Louth identifies the unitive core of the concept: "Redemption is essentially an act of God's love for humankind, love which is essentially unitive, and the purpose of this love is not just to make amends for human sin, or even simply to heal wounds inflicted by sin and death, but to draw the human—and through the human the whole created cosmos—into union with God, which entails deification."[39] God's redemptive love draws hu-mans, together with the entire creation, into union with him; this is the purpose of God's salvific mission. In the unitive understanding of salvation, salvation is about becoming a participant in the com-munion of the Father, the Son, and the Holy Spirit. Such participation in the life of the Trinity is what worship (*leitourgia*) in Orthodox

---

Kärkkäinen, "Deification View," in *Justification: Five Views*, ed. James K. Beilby and Paul Rhodes Eddy (Downers Grove, IL: IVP Academic, 2011), 219–43. Some Reformed theologians have also found deification in John Calvin's teaching. Michael Horton quotes Calvin as saying that "'deification' is 'the greatest possible bless-ing.'" See Horton, "Response to Andrew Louth," in *Five Views on the Extent of the Atonement*, ed. Adam J. Johnson, Counterpoints: Bible & Theology (Grand Rapids: Zondervan Academic, 2019), 53.

36. Lossky, "Redemption and Deification," 98.

37. Stephen Finland and Vladimir Kharlamov, introduction to *Theōsis: Deifica-tion in Christian Theology*, ed. S. Finlan and V. Kharlamov (Portland, OR: Wipf & Stock, 2006), 2.

38. Alister McGrath, *Christian Theology: An Introduction*, 2nd ed. (Oxford: Blackwell, 1997), 414.

39. Andrew Louth, "Eastern Orthodox View," in *Five Views on the Extent of the Atonement*, ed. Adam J. Johnson, Counterpoints: Bible & Theology (Grand Rapids: Zondervan Academic, 2019), 36–37.

theology is about. Referring to the role of worship in the revived patristic theology, Ciprian Streza makes a relevant comment. He says that patristic theology "views the liturgy as the communion of eternal love between the persons of the Holy Trinity, a communion that all creatures are called to be immersed in through grace, a communion that was . . . made available to all Christians through the Savior's crucifixion and resurrection, and through the Holy Spirit's descent and activity inside the Church."[40] The keyword here is "communion" which, "rather than any other juridical and rationalistic model," according to Orthodox theologian John Meyendorff, "was adequate for the Orthodox view of 'life in Christ' and salvation."[41] Meyendorff continues, "The concept of communion with God or deification (*theosis*) . . . was used to define the authentic human destiny and . . . the purpose of man's creation by God" in Greek patristic thought.[42]

Somewhat similar yet quite different is the salvific understanding drawn in connection to a conception in Hinduism's Upanishad text (the last of the Vedic texts). We name this "oneness with God" to distinguish it from the previous concept discussed and because of the monistic (or nondualistic) philosophy behind it. We include it here to illustrate the continuing multiplication of salvific theories in the global church today. The Upanishadic conception is best explicated in a philosophy known as Advaita Vedanta (nondualistic interpretation of the Upanishad). Often known as the scholastic philosophy of Hinduism advanced by the brilliant teacher Shankara, Advaita Vedanta interprets the Upanishadic texts to mean that salvation (moksha, or liberation) consists in the union of the true self (atman) with the ultimate reality (Brahman).[43] The famous Upanishad phrase "Atman is Brahman" is interpreted to mean that the true self of the individual (atman) is one and the same with the ultimate reality or the cosmic soul (Brahman).[44]

40. Ciprian Ioan Streza, "The Divine Liturgy in Orthodox Spirituality: The Mystery of Man's Personal Encounter with God through Worship and Ascetical Life," *Greek Orthodox Theological Review* 58 (2013): 142.

41. John Meyendorff, "New Life in Christ: Salvation in Orthodox Theology," *Theological Studies* 50 (1989): 484.

42. Meyendorff, "New Life in Christ," 489.

43. See, e.g., Klaus K. Klostermaier, *A Survey of Hinduism*, 3rd ed. (Albany: State University of New York, 2007), 355–59.

44. Klostermaier, *Survey of Hinduism*, 166–72.

In other words, "the self of a person is identical with the ground of all being."[45] The realization of this oneness is the salvific enlightenment in which the individual comes to realize the eternity of his or her being. This school of thought was most popular in modern Hindu reform and most influential among modern Hindu intellectuals, including converts to Christianity. For some Christians of Hindu background, the divine-human unity of Christ, which they often closely related to the atman-Brahman identification, is deeply salvific. Raimon Panikkar, who is emphatic on the universality of Christ and his salvation, sees Christ symbolically ("Christophany") as the universal salvific fullness of humanity, or the entire creation.[46] As a way of expressing Christ's mystical union of the divine and human, he constructs terms like "theandrism" (God-man) and "cosmotheandrism" (the unity of humanity, God, and the cosmos).[47] If Panikkar is overly symbolic at the expense of a historical Jesus, as many Christian scholars charge,[48] another Advaitic theologian, Brahmabandhab Upadhyay,[49] is closer to historic Christianity. In the period of his life when he was most active in theological interpretation, Upadhyay stated that "the only way . . . to salvation, is to be one with God who compassionates us by superimposing upon Himself sorrow and suffering for our transgressions."[50] Such a statement may be seen as what Timothy Tennent calls an attempt to harmonize Shankara's Advaita with Thomistic theology.[51] After a long struggle, Upadhyay shifted from resisting to advocating Advaitic philosophy as a hermeneutical tool for Christianity and interpreted "Atman is Brahman" in Christian theological terms.[52]

45. Klostermaier, *Survey of Hinduism*, 357.

46. Raimon Panikkar, *Christophany: The Fullness of Man* (Maryknoll, NY: Orbis Books, 2004).

47. See, e.g., Jyri Komulainen, *An Emerging Cosmotheandric Religion? Raimon Panikkar's Pluralistic Theology of Religions* (Leiden: Brill, 2005), 128–30.

48. See, e.g., M. M. Thomas, *Risking Christ for Christ's Sake: Toward an Ecumenical Theology of Pluralism* (Geneva: World Council of Churches, 1987), 106–8.

49. For a detailed and analytical discussion, see Timothy C. Tennent, *Building Christianity on Indian Foundations: The Legacy of Brahmabāndhav Upādhyāy* (Delhi: ISPCK, 2000), 274–82.

50. Brahmabandhab Upadhyay, "Christ's Claims to Attention," in *The Writings of Brahmabandhab Upadhyay*, ed. Julius Lipner and George Gispert-Sauch (Bangalore: The United Theological College, 1991), 195.

51. Tennent, *Building Christianity*, 256.

52. Tennent, *Building Christianity*, 274–82.

Salvation as New or Renewed Life

Many terms are available for this topic, but each has the potential to limit the meaning. In addition to "new life" and "renewal of life," terms like "restoration," "revitalization," "restitution," "rejuvenation," and "regeneration" have been used, but they all have their particular uses and potentially fail to express the broad meaning we intend here. While recognizing the possibility of limiting the meaning, we are also bound to pick a term. The intent is to say that God's salvation is about God's gift of life, and such a gift may come as a renewal of life. The goal is to restore life as he first intended it at creation—that is, to restore human beings in his image and all creation as it was intended to be. This renewal of life has been variously articulated and interpreted, including "humanization" with Christ as the new human.[53] Our emphasis here is on God's gift and renewal of life. Thus, we group together (1) new birth, which refers particularly to the human experience of renewed life, and (2) restoration of creation. Restoration of life is as much a gift of new life as it is a renewal and restoration. God's gift of new life to fallen humanity may broadly be defined as work to renew or regenerate life. From a recipient's viewpoint, it may be a new birth or a rebirth from above, as stated in John 3:3. While it is impossible to separate the notion of God's gift from its reception by human beings in the discussion, our emphasis here is on the giving side of the equation. Salvation is God's gift of new life. Yet the discussion will have to go back and forth between the giving and receiving of new life since it is the reception that makes clear the gift. With this in mind, we discuss the idea of salvation as God's gift of new life with the topics of new birth and new creation.

The idea of the new birth is drawn mainly from John's Gospel and Paul's Letters, where the idea of salvation as gaining new life in Jesus Christ is dominant. Most well known is a passage in John where Jesus tells Nicodemus that new birth is necessary to see the kingdom of God (John 3:3). The Greek term used is *anōthen*, which has a double meaning of "from above" and "again or anew." The

---

53. M. M. Thomas, *Salvation and Humanisation* (Madras, India: The Christian Literature Society, 1971).

apparent meaning is the new birth, but the meaning has at least two senses. As Gail R. O'Day helpfully points out, "'To be born *anōthen*' speaks both of a time of birth ('again') and the place from which this new birth is generated ('from above')."[54] So, the newness is both temporal and spatial. The same double sense can be applied to the kingdom of God in that the kingdom of God is about time and place.[55] At one level, it signifies the eschatological (end-time) nature of the teaching. At another, it shows the newness and power of the source of the new birth—namely, God's Spirit.

Since the onset of the evangelical revival in the 1730s, the topic of new birth has been associated with evangelicalism.[56] While most evangelists today give sweeping treatment even to the point of making it a slogan,[57] a few have given more analytical treatment. For some, it is the experiential aspect of being justified by God. Others use it interchangeably with justification.[58] When salvation (as God's work) and conversion (as the outcome of salvation in human beings) are differentiated, "new birth" is often treated as equivalent to conversion. This should not lead to discounting the work of God's Spirit in the latter. No one gave so prominent a place to this theme in modern Christianity as John Wesley.[59] While closely relating it to justification, Wesley also distinguishes it. He begins his sermon "New Birth" (1760) by saying, "If any doctrines within the whole compass of Christianity may be properly termed fundamental, they are doubtless these two,—the doctrine of justification, and that of the new birth: The former relating to that great work which God does for us, in forgiving our sins;

54. Gail R. O'Day, "The Gospel of John: Introduction, Commentary, and Reflection," in *The New Interpreter's Bible*, ed. Leander E. Keck (Nashville: Abingdon Press, 1995), 9:549.

55. O'Day, "Gospel of John," 9:549.

56. For a good treatment on the topic among two famous leaders of the evangelical revival, George Whitefield and John Wesley, see Timothy L. Smith, *Whitefield and Wesley on the New Birth* (Grand Rapids: Francis Asbury, 1986).

57. By turning it into a slogan, interpreters "domesticate the radical newness of Jesus' words and diminish the good news," warns O'Day. O'Day, "Gospel of John," 9:555.

58. See, e.g., the prominent preacher Billy Graham, *Peace with God* (Nashville: W Publishing Group, 1984), chap. 12.

59. For a collection of his sermons and reflections on the topic, see John Wesley, *The New Birth*, ed. Thomas C. Oden (San Francisco: Harper & Row, 1984).

the latter, to the great work which God does in us, in renewing our fallen nature."[60] To Wesley, these two are fundamentally important in the Christian faith. God's work "for us" and God's work "in us" may be understood as complementary sides of the same coin. Treating new birth as God's work in and with us is of special significance in this study. To Wesley, while justification and new birth are very close to each other, they do have "logical" distinctions.[61] Chronologically, "neither of these is before the other: in the moment we are justified by the grace of God, through the redemption that is in Jesus, we are also 'born of the Spirit,'" he said. Yet, "in order of thinking," he continues, "justification precedes the new birth. We first conceive his wrath to be turned away, and then his Spirit to work in our hearts."[62]

In Wesley's rich teaching on the new birth or regeneration, the topic of "entire sanctification" is distinct and controversial. It is also considered to be Wesley's most misunderstood teaching.[63] In his close study of Wesley's teaching on the new birth, Kenneth Collins shows that Wesley believed that there are two or more "degrees of regeneration."[64] As the work of God's Spirit "in us," regeneration can reach a perfect degree, so to speak. This "perfect sense of regeneration for Wesley," according to Collins, "is to have 'total freedom' from all the stirrings and motions of sin."[65] This total freedom is what Wesley calls "entire sanctification."[66] While the expression "entire sanctification" has met with opposition from other Christian confessional bodies, as the work of the omnipotent sovereign God "in us," the teaching does make sense.

Pope Francis says, "Eternal life will be a shared experience of awe, in which each creature, resplendently transfigured, will take

60. John Wesley, "The New Birth," sermon 45 of *The Sermons of John Wesley*, ed. Michael Anderson with corrections by Ryan Danker and George Lyons, Wesley Center for Applied Theology, Wesley Center Online, accessed April 30, 2020, http://wesley.nnu.edu/John-wesley/the-sermons-of-john-wesley-1872-edition/sermon-45-the-new-birth/.

61. Collins, *Scripture Way of Salvation*, 105.

62. Wesley, "New Birth."

63. For an example of the debate on the topic, see Melvin E. Dieter et al., *Five Views on Sanctification* (Grand Rapids: Zondervan, 1987).

64. Collins, *Scripture Way of Salvation*, 107.

65. Collins, *Scripture Way of Salvation*, 107.

66. Collins, *Scripture Way of Salvation*, 108.

its rightful place and have something to give those poor men and women who will have been liberated once and for all."[67] With the rise of ecotheology resulting from environmental awareness, we are discovering the relationship between salvation of human beings and salvation of the creation. There has been an important movement in Christian soteriology from being very anthropocentric to being cosmic, emphatically including the entire creation in the realm of God's salvation. Furthermore, we have realized the integration of humanity and creation in the mission of God. In this light, the World Council of Churches' ecumenical affirmation on missions and evangelism titled "Together Towards Life"[68] is significant. Although its reference to "life" is often vague,[69] its affirmation of the interconnectedness of human life with other forms of life is unambiguous. On salvation, the statement says, "God did not send the Son for the salvation of humanity alone or give us partial salvation. Rather the gospel is the good news for every part of creation and every aspect of our life and society. It is therefore vital to recognize God's mission in a cosmic sense and to affirm all life, the whole *oikoumene*, as being interconnected in God's web of life."[70]

Many biblical scholars and theologians around the world have been rereading biblical teachings on creation and engaging what has come to be called ecotheology, a constructive theology focusing on nature especially in the light of environmental concerns. Developing contextual theologies in Asia[71] have great potential for an ecologically conscious understanding of salvation, and the salvation

67. Francis, Laudato si': *Encyclical Letter of the Holy Father Francis on Care for Our Common Home*, May 24, 2015 (Vatican: Vatican Press, 2015), sec. 243, https://w2.vatican.va/content/dam/francesco/pdf/encyclicals/documents/papa-francesco_20150524_enciclica-laudato-si_en.pdf.

68. Jooseop Keum, ed., *Together towards Life: Mission and Evangelism in Changing Landscapes; with a Practical Guide* (Geneva: World Council of Churches, 2013) https://www.oikoumene.org/en/resources/publications/TogethertowardsLife_Missionand Evangelism.pdf.

69. It does not distinguish between old and new or sinful and redeemed. While its emphasis on life renewed by the Holy Spirit seems to affirm newness of life, its celebration and affirmation of all lives is confusing.

70. Keum, *Together towards Life*, 5.

71. See, e.g., the argument for potential creation theology by Po Ho Huang, "Towards a Paradigm Shift in Theology: From Euro-Andro-Anthropocentric Salvation to the Redemption of God's Creation," *Theologies and Cultures* 8, no. 1 (June 2011): 8–27.

conception of grassroots African Independent Christianity has a lot to teach the world church about "earthkeeping."[72] A powerful theology of creation in recent years comes from the theology of Indigenous people, whose strong connection to the land as a part of their cultural identity gives them spiritual wisdom to share on the topic.[73] One such example comes from Native American (or First Nation) theology. Using the "Native American well-being as a harmony construction"[74] to understand biblical shalom, Native American theologian Randy Woodley shows how "the Creator is calling us [the human community] back to experience God's love and care in the created world."[75] The emerging voices of Eastern Orthodox theologians and their "patristic revival,"[76] especially the soteriology of *theosis* we have discussed, also contribute to this new conception of salvation. By treating salvation of creation under three theories—namely, the renewal of the creation, the restoration of the creation, and Christ the goal of creation—Peter Schmiechen clearly emphasizes this topic.[77]

The title of Howard Snyder's work, "Salvation Means Creation Healed,"[78] is a clarifying statement of salvation as the renewal of creation. Snyder, along with Joel Scandrett, argues that Christianity has wrongly divorced the earth from heaven, and consequently, the

---

72. M. L. Daneel, "AIC Pneumatology and the Salvation of All Creation," in *All Things Hold Together: Holistic Theologies at the African Grassroots* (Pretoria: University of South Africa, 2007), 21–45.

73. By considering their traditional perspectives on land and the earth, some tribal theologians in India have made theological reflections on ecotheology. See, e.g., Wati Longchar, *Returning to Mother Earth: Theology, Christian Witness and Theological Education; An Indigenous Perspective* (Tainan, Taiwan: Programme for Theology and Cultures in Asia, 2012), 43–68; Hrangthan Chhungi, "Heritage of the Tribal Religious Practices in India: An Ecological Concern," in *Theologizing Tribal Heritage: A Critical Re-look*, ed. Hrangthan Chhungi (Delhi: ISPCK, 2012), 157–70.

74. Randy S. Woodley, *Shalom and the Community of Creation: An Indigenous Vision* (Grand Rapids: Eerdmans, 2012), xv.

75. Woodley, *Shalom and the Community*, xix.

76. Meyendorff, "New Life in Christ," 485–86.

77. Schmiechen, *Saving Power*, 169–252.

78. Howard Snyder, "Salvation Means Creation Healed: Creation, Cross, Kingdom, and Mission," *Asbury Journal* 62, no. 1 (2007): 9–47; cf. Howard Snyder with Joel Scandrett, *Salvation Means Creation Healed: The Ecology of Sin and Grace* (Eugene, OR: Cascade Books, 2011).

salvation image came to exclude the earth. In contrast, they reason that salvation means the restoration or healing of the entire creation. "The plan (economy) of salvation pictured in texts like Ephesians 1, Colossians 1, and Hebrew 1 is this: *that God may glorify himself by reconciling all things in Jesus Christ.* The biblical vision is of all the earth's people, and in fact all creation, united in praising and serving God."[79] Challenging some popular assumptions about life after death, including the Christian notion of the otherness of heaven from the earth, N. T. Wright asserts that redemption is the remaking of the entire creation. Wright firmly resists the influence of (1) modernist-progressivism, which fails to deal with evil in the world, and (2) the escapist theory of spiritualists drawn from Platonic Gnosticism.[80] Then, he reintroduces the Christian faith in the future resurrection, reinterpreting Christian hope in the new heaven and new earth by wedding together heaven and earth. He writes, "Redemption is not simply making creation a bit better, as the optimistic evolutionist would try to suggest. Nor is it rescuing spirits and souls from an evil material world, as the Gnostic would want to say. It is the remaking of creation, having dealt with the evil that is defacing and distorting it. And it is accomplished by the same God, now known in Jesus Christ, through whom it was made in the first place."[81]

Salvation as "creation healed" (Snyder) and "the remaking of creation" (Wright) does not disparage the place and role of the human. The most important biblical text on the salvation of creation is Romans 8:18–21. Although just three or four verses, this text's clarity and emphatic expression make it all the more important: "For I consider that the sufferings of this present time are not worth comparing with the glory that is to be revealed to us. For the creation waits with eager longing for the revealing of the sons of God. For the creation was subjected to futility, not willingly, but because of him who subjected it, in hope that the creation itself will be set free

79. Snyder with Scandrett, *Salvation Means Creation Healed*, 99 (emphasis original).

80. N. T. Wright, *Surprised by Hope: Rethinking Heaven, the Resurrection, and the Mission of the Church* (New York: HarperCollins, 2008), 81–91.

81. N. T. Wright, *Surprised by Hope*, 97.

from its bondage to corruption and obtain the freedom of the glory of the children of God" (ESV).

This passage shows the global and cosmic dimension of God's salvation in connection with the salvation of human beings. While attempts have been made to read the passage as centering on creation, even seeing the center to be "mother earth" giving birth to God's children,[82] the text explicitly maintains the primacy of human beings in the chain of salvation. The creation's freedom is dependent on "the freedom of the glory of the children of God." The immensity of the glory to be revealed, for Paul, is such that "the whole creation is on tiptoe with excitement."[83] What is this glory? What does "revealing of the children of God" mean? N. T. Wright uses continuity-discontinuity tension to explain the meaning. Paul's expression in the passage suggests that this revelation "is not [a mere] unmaking of creation or simply its steady development but the drastic and dramatic birth of new creation from the womb of the old."[84] By rejecting the notion that the new creation will discard the old and the present earth will be cast off, these theologians see the renewal of the entire creation as part of biblical redemption.

To briefly summarize our discussion of the various theories and motifs of salvation, we proposed integrating different theories of salvation under four main categories. The first one, the liberational notion connected to the triumphal work of God, shows the revolutionary nature of salvation. It appeals more to marginalized and subjugated communities who are looking for deliverance from their bondage. The salvation perspectives that employ redemption imagery, our second group, offer rationalistic and forensic explanations. From this perspective, salvation is about righting the wrong and recovering the wronged to the rightful place. The third group shows that salvation is not only related to objective works of God but it includes humans being drawn to and united with God. Paul's language of reconciliation with God and with one another connects salvation with

82. Courtney J. P. Friesen, "Birthing the Children of God: Echoes of Theogony in Romans 8:19–23," *New Testament Studies* 63, no. 2 (April 2007): 246–60.
83. N. T. Wright, "The Letter to the Romans: Introduction, Commentary, and Reflections," in *The New Interpreter's Bible*, ed. Leander E. Keck (Nashville: Abingdon Press, 2002), 10:596.
84. N. T. Wright, *Surprised by Hope*, 104.

the idea of peace. Understanding salvation as union with God seems to appeal most to Eurasians of Eastern Orthodox and Brahmanic Hindu backgrounds. According to the fourth group, the basic motif of salvation is about saving the dying and giving new life, renewing a fading and waning life.

Each of these four blocks of salvific images consists of a variety of images and metaphors, and together they show the richness of biblical soteriology. We attempt here to integrate these theories in a meaningful way. The richness of the metaphors and the variety of the theories have helped keep the theme of salvation alive and meaningful for the church in different periods and places throughout its history. As we reflect on the church's history in its dealing with the idea of salvation, we consider it fortunate that the church did not canonize any particular theory or make any particular dogmatic statement on salvation. Christians of different times, regions, and cultures have used different models to understand God's gift of salvation.

The Scope of Salvation and the Theology of Religions

Between the Universal Saving Will of God and the Salvific Decisiveness of Christ

Jesus's answer to the disciples' question "Who can be saved?" puts to rest the question of "can" by confirming that only God can save (Matt. 19:25–26). However, the question of who *will* be saved remains open even after two millennia. The question of who will be included and what includes them in God's salvation in Jesus Christ has been debated in different ways throughout Christian history. Summarizing this long debate, McGrath says that two "central assumptions" have controlled it, both of which are well grounded in the New Testament. They are "the affirmation of the universal saving will of God" and "the affirmation that salvation is possible only in and through Christ."[85] Naming these two important "truths" of Christianity, Indian theologian O. V. Jathanna also asserts that "any Christian theology worth its name should hold together" these two—namely,

---

85. McGrath, *Christian Theology: An Introduction*, 417.

the universal salvific will of God and the decisiveness of Christ.[86] When taken to their extremes, one leads to salvation of all (universalism) as God's will, and the other narrowly restricts salvation to those who explicitly affirm Jesus as their savior. While passages such as Acts 4:12 and John 14:16 surely affirm Jesus as the only savior, God's will to save everyone is clear in passages such as 1 Timothy 2:4 and 2 Peter 3:9. Among Protestants, beyond restricting salvation to those who know, believe, and explicitly affirm Jesus Christ as the savior, some firmly believe in God's election of the few for salvation. On the opposite end, Christians who understand God primarily in terms of his love cannot narrowly set the extent of salvation.

For Christians in societies with a long history of the Christian faith, the contradistinction between the two orientations may not be immediately apparent. They may not see any issue in affirming salvation through Jesus Christ as the way God intends to save everyone. On the other hand, for new Christians in societies with no prior knowledge of the gospel and Christianity, the fate of their forebears' souls, those who died before hearing the gospel, can be an unrelenting question. When such questions arise, they often result in heated debates. Gabriel Fackre tells the story of nineteenth-century Hawaiian converts who asked their Congregationalist missionaries from Boston, "What will happen to our ancestors of blessed memories? They never heard the good news."[87] The missionaries brought the question back to Boston, and theologians, clergy, and laity had such a heated debate in churches and institutions that even a New York magazine covered the story at that time.[88] Because the question is so difficult and the issue so sensitive, many Christians in the Global South seem to have swept it under the rug. Confronted explicitly with the question "Do you believe that your great-grandfather was condemned to hell because he did not know the gospel?" they often lose their firmness of conviction. In societies where Christians are a

86. Origen Vasantha Jathanna, *The Decisiveness of the Christ-Event and the Universality of Christianity in a World of Religious Plurality* (Bern, Switzerland: Peter Lang, 1981), 436.

87. Gabriel Fackre, "Divine Perseverance," in *What about Those Who Have Never Heard? Three Views on the Destiny of the Unevangelized*, ed. John Sanders (Downers Grove, IL: InterVarsity, 1995), 71.

88. Fackre, "Divine Perseverance," 71.

minority and often live with close non-Christian relatives and loved ones, a very restrictive understanding of salvation may look not only untenable but unreal.

We can identify at least two major circles of Christian debate on salvation's scope or extent during the past fifty years, and we do so within their theologies of religions. The first one is the pluralism debate, spearheaded by scholars who identify themselves as "pluralists." The second circle of the debate involves what may broadly be called the fate of the unevangelized, debated intensely by those who explicitly identify themselves as "evangelicals." The pluralism debate came about in connection with the salvation of non-Christians and was framed clearly as a theology of religions. While pluralists gave the teachings and adherents of world religions the most prominent role, the main question came down to the scope of salvation in the Christian faith: Can the followers of non-Christian religions be saved? Can the teachings of other religions save their adherents? Such questions ultimately lead to the question "Is Jesus the only savior?" These questions may surprise and even trouble Christians who regard all non-Christians to be damned to hell. Pluralists raise these questions to challenge traditional and evangelical Christians who mostly regard salvation as only possible through explicit faith in Jesus Christ. As the basis of their argument, they unapologetically refer to the increasingly globalized world, where people of different faiths mingle in the same cultures. In their attempts to find a place for other faiths within Christian teaching, pluralists largely set aside the traditional Christian claim of having the one and only savior of the world. Some question crucial doctrines of Christianity, such as the incarnation,[89] while others reinterpret some key biblical texts.

The group relied heavily on a way of categorizing every Christian as holding an exclusive, an inclusive, or their new pluralist view on people of other (non-Christian) religions.[90] Despite the variety of

89. John Hick, *The Metaphor of God Incarnate: Christology in a Pluralistic Age*, 2nd ed. (Louisville: Westminster John Knox, 2006). Here Hick argues that Jesus did not really understand himself to be God incarnate and that the doctrine of incarnation should be accepted as "a metaphorical idea" (p. 12).

90. Alan Race crafted this list first in his book *Christians and Religious Pluralism: Patterns in the Christian Theology of Religions* (Maryknoll, NY: Orbis Books, 1982).

their approaches—which range from an insistence on a godlike (ultimate) reality across religions (John Hick) to a liberation approach (Knitter) to a mystery-centered theocentricity (Samartha)—they do have some strong shared voices. These pluralists sought to move from a Christocentric Christianity to a vaguely defined theocentric Christianity, presenting their theology as the pinnacle of progress in the attitude toward other religions. The group met at Claremont Graduate School in California in March 1986 and produced a book that testifies to the unity of their voices.[91] They strongly rejected approaches they called "the 'conservative' *exclusivist*," according to which there is "salvation only in Christ," and "the 'liberal' *inclusivist*," which they said expects the salvifically rich teaching of other religions to be fulfilled in Jesus Christ, the redeemer. These pluralists claimed to have found "the independent validity of other [religious] ways,"[92] which, they say, is "the crossing of a theological Rubicon."[93]

Of course, there are biblical texts standing in the way of this claim for the validity of other religions' teachings, especially those texts that attest that Jesus is the one and only savior. Some pluralists have taken the time to deal with and question Jesus's claim to be the only way to God the Father (John 14:6) and the apostle Peter's insistence that there is no other name besides Jesus able to bring salvation (Acts 4:12).[94] At the heart of their argument against Christian exclusivism is the question of the uniqueness and finality of Jesus Christ. Some explicitly reject his uniqueness, and others reinterpret it to limit its scope.

While pluralists have made their case in multiple ways, their theology has also received much criticism and rejection. Many orthodox Christians rebuff pluralists' claims and viewpoints as a way of

---

91. John Hick and Paul F. Knitter, eds., *The Myth of Christian Uniqueness: Toward a Pluralistic Theology of Religions*, Faith Meets Faith Series (Maryknoll, NY: Orbis Books, 1987).

92. Knitter, preface to *Myth of Christian Uniqueness*, by Hick and Knitter, viii.

93. Knitter, preface to *Myth of Christian Uniqueness*, by Hick and Knitter, viii.

94. For instance, see Paul F. Knitter, *Jesus and the Other Names: Christian Mission and Global Responsibility* (Maryknoll, NY: Orbis Books, 1996), 69–72; Stanley J. Samartha, *One Christ—Many Religions: Toward a Revised Christology* (Bangalore: SATHRI, 1992), 94–102.

surrendering Christian uniqueness to the pressure of multireligiosity. Some simply reject the theology as un-Christian for its reduction of Christ's role, while others question the logic of the theological arguments. Some observers allege that pluralists are as exclusivist as the exclusivists they condemn. One may also wonder if they fail to respect other religions' independence and uniqueness when they equate their various paths of salvation.[95]

Questions surrounding salvation and the unevangelized began to swirl among evangelicals in the early 1990s. The publication of the book *Through No Fault of Their Own* in 1991,[96] for instance, signaled this new momentum. More than twenty contributors took up the challenge of pluralism and universalism and dealt with various biblical and theological themes connected to the issue. Even while some of the pluralists' contentions were dismissed as un-Christian on the basis of the Christian faith tradition, evangelicals who believe Jesus is the only savior and who look to the Bible as the authoritative source of faith still disagree on how one receives salvation and who all will be saved. The emergence of evangelical inclusivists has enhanced this new cycle of debate among evangelicals, though the questions they pose are not new. Some of the positions taken are either renewed or reinterpreted from the past. In his doctoral dissertation at the University of Basel in the late 1970s, Jathanna dealt with what he called "the *ante Jesum Christum natum* problem" (the question of salvation before the time of Jesus Christ) and outlined various theological arguments.[97] The debate among evangelicals renewed the issue with fresh approaches, and new terms were coined to refine old ideas, including accessibilism,[98] particularism, and restrictivism. As will be shown later, the debate helped clarify the

95. For one of the best critical assessment of pluralists' soteriology, see S. Mark Heim, *Salvations: Truth and Difference in Religions* (Maryknoll, NY: Orbis Books, 1995), 13–126.

96. William V. Crockett and James G. Sigountos, eds., *Through No Fault of Their Own? The Fate of Those Who Have Never Heard* (Grand Rapids: Baker, 1991).

97. Jathanna, *Decisiveness of the Christ-Event*, 436–64.

98. On this term, see Terrance L. Tiessen, *Who Can Be Saved? Reassessing Salvation in Christ and World Religions* (Downers Grove, IL: InterVarsity, 2004), 33, 40–42, 48–72.

positions of those variously called exclusivists, restrictivists, and
particularists.

With their publications in 1992, Clark Pinnock[99] and John Sanders[100] brought greater awareness to this new evangelical inclusivism
under a position called "the wider hope," an expression coined a century earlier.[101] Both carefully articulate the evangelical nature of their
positions by affirming—to use Pinnock's words—"the unbounded
generosity of God revealed in Jesus Christ"[102] and advocating "salvation optimism" through "a hermeneutic of hopefulness."[103] Pinnock's is primarily a theological-hermeneutical argument, whereas
Sanders combines historical survey with theological argument. With
his core question of the destiny of the unevangelized, Sanders positions "the wider hope" viewpoint between "restrictivism" (a term
he introduced), which says, "All the unevangelized are damned,"[104]
and "universalism," which says, "All the unevangelized are saved."[105]
He locates his inclusive soteriology within "the wider hope" position, arguing that salvation is universally accessible even without
evangelization.[106] His categorization and labeling are quite general
and may even appear simplistic, but he makes a clear argument for
an evangelical inclusivism position. Other evangelicals of different
ecclesiastical backgrounds follow the path of Pinnock and Sanders.
Terrance Tiessen, for instance, has made a well-sustained argument
for inclusivistic soteriology from a Reformed perspective.[107]

Corresponding to the threefold typology of the Christian approach to other religions (exclusivism, inclusivism, and pluralism),
the evangelical debate on the fate of the unevangelized also tends to

99. Clark Pinnock, *A Wideness in God's Mercy: The Finality of Jesus Christ in
a World of Religions* (Grand Rapids: Zondervan, 1992).

100. John Sanders, *No Other Name: An Investigation into the Destination of the
Unevangelized* (Grand Rapids: Eerdmans, 1992).

101. See Fredric William Farrar, Thomas de Quincy, and James Hogg, *The Wider
Hope: Essays and Strictures on the Doctrine and Literature of Future Punishment*
(New York: Dutton, 1890).

102. Pinnock, *Wideness in God's Mercy*, 18.

103. Pinnock, *Wideness in God's Mercy*, 20.

104. Sanders, *No Other Name*, 37–51.

105. Sanders, *No Other Name*, 81–98.

106. Sanders, *No Other Name*, 215–69.

107. Tiessen, *Who Can Be Saved?*

consolidate into three main positions. Nevertheless, the three positions are named differently depending on the emphasis given. As seen above, in attempting to highlight his own inclusive position as a middle path, Sanders named them restrictivism, inclusivism, and universalism. Sanders also initiated a three-way debate with Gabriel Fackre, who held "divine perseverance," and Ronald Nash, who defended "restrictivism."[108] Taking the conservative Reformed view of the so-called limited atonement into consideration, McGrath identifies the three positions as "all will be saved" (universalism), "only believers will be saved," and "only the elect will be saved" (particular redemption).[109] McGrath includes what Sanders calls "inclusivism" as a modified form of salvation of the believers.[110]

In one of the earliest evangelical projects on salvation with respect to religious pluralism, the book *Four Views on Salvation in a Pluralistic World* assembles some of the finest articulations of the various viewpoints.[111] The project adapts the three categories (exclusivism, inclusivism, and pluralism), replacing exclusivism with two views on "particularism." The deliberate replacement of exclusivism with particularism (emphasizing the particularity of the Christian concept of salvation in Christ)[112] and the inclusion of two different particularist views (post-Enlightenment and evidentialist) can be seen as an evangelical statement opposing the label of exclusivism and recognizing the diversity within evangelicalism. The book produces a stimulating debate on salvation among pluralist (John Hick), inclusivist (Clark Pinnock), and particularist (post-Enlightenment

---

108. John Sanders, *What about Those Who Have Never Heard?*
109. McGrath, *Christian Theology: An Introduction*, 417–20. A debate within conservative Reformed circles further shows three main viewpoints as "definite atonement" (particular, limited), "general atonement" (which is "universal in intention and provisional in character"), and "a multi-intentions view of the atonement" (which argues for "both universal and particular purposes" and provisional and efficacious characters). See Andrew David Naselli and Mark Snoeberger, eds., *Perspectives on the Extent of the Atonement: Three Views* (Nashville: B&H, 2015).
110. McGrath, *Christian Theology: An Introduction*, 419.
111. Dennis L. Okholm and Timothy R. Phillips, eds., *Four Views on Salvation in a Pluralistic World* (Secunderabad, India: OM Books, 2001). The book was originally published as *More Than One Way?* (Grand Rapids: Zondervan, 1995). I use the Indian edition, which was published in cooperation with the original publisher, Zondervan.
112. Okholm and Phillips, introduction to *Four Views on Salvation*, 16–17.

by Alister McGrath; evidentialist by Douglas Geivett and Gary Phillips) viewpoints.

Most studies on the historical discussions of the scope of salvation acknowledge the multiplicity of viewpoints, perhaps as many as eight positions.[113] While every Christian denomination changes over time and may include different viewpoints, most Protestant denominations originated with a particular soteriology. As mentioned before, a soteriological understanding and approach often serve as confessional and denominational foundations, especially among Protestants after the Reformation in the sixteenth century. In his studies on Christian attitudes and theologies of religions, Paul Knitter combines confessional and denominational identities as theological markers, while recognizing progressive endeavors to be mainly individual ventures.[114] Debating the extent of the atonement from a confessional-denominational viewpoint, the book by Andrew Louth (Eastern Orthodox), Matthew Levering (Roman Catholic), Michael Horton (traditional Reformed), Fred Sanders (Wesleyan), and Tom Greggs (Christian Universalist) shows soteriological stances of different confessional traditions in an engaging way.[115] While the Roman Catholic, Reformed, Wesleyan, and universalist soteriologies are relatively familiar, the presentations on Eastern Orthodox's universalism and Christianity's universalism are bold and fresh.

As mentioned, theologians Jathanna and McGrath identify two seemingly opposed biblical points, and they suggest neither be surrendered to the other: the universal saving will of God and the particularity of salvation in Christ. How one holds the two "truths" (Jathanna) together determines one's view on the scope of salvation. Theologians have struggled to keep these two points in tension. The

113. John Sanders listed as many as eight different positions. See Sanders, introduction to *What about Those Who Have Never Heard?*, 13–15.
114. In his 1985 and 2002 books, he uses evangelical Christianity (total replacement), mainline Protestant or the World Council of Churches (partial replacement), post-Vatican-II Catholic (fulfillment), and individual progressive scholars (mutuality and acceptance) as theological markers of the different models he outlined. See Paul F. Knitter, *No Other Name? A Critical Survey of Christian Attitudes toward the World Religions* (Maryknoll, NY: Orbis Books, 1985); and Paul F. Knitter, *Introducing Theologies of Religions* (Maryknoll, NY: Orbis Books, 2002).
115. Johnson, *Five Views*.

problem with universalism is that it assumes the saving will of God to mean "all must be saved." What about those who would not believe or do not want to be saved? "Universalism" in the end, as McGrath points out, "denies humanity the right to say no to God." The biblical testimony seems clear in that God does not insist but offers us salvation, which can be refused. But the problem with restricting salvation to the conscious confession of faith is the presence of passages in the Bible that show God's will to save all and the possibility of acquiring Christ's salvation without knowing Christ's name personally.

In Three Soteriological Positions

Suppose we use these three main soteriological positions to represent groups of viewpoints and recognize that each group consists of multiple viewpoints. This allows us to pull them together in a sensible manner. First, we have the most popular and traditional position, variously called restrictivism, exclusivism, and particularism. We may safely retain the name inclusivism for the middle position, while acknowledging differences under the nomenclature. The third and most progressive view we will call universalism, especially as we discuss the extent or scope of the Christian understanding of salvation. I will discuss inclusivist soteriology last as the final and pivotal point in the following discussion.

Restrictive-Particularism

The six-point "set of beliefs" outlined by Millard Erickson as "the traditional view of Christianity"—that is, Western Protestant Christianity—largely summarizes the traditional exclusive or restrictive understanding of salvation:

1. All humans are sinners, by nature and by choice, and are therefore guilty and under divine condemnation.
2. Salvation is only through Christ and his atoning work.
3. Belief is necessary to obtain the salvation achieved by Christ. Therefore, Christians and the church have a responsibility to tell unbelievers the good news about Jesus Christ.
4. Adherents of other religions, no matter how sincere their belief . . . are spiritually lost apart from Christ.

5. Physical death brings to an end the opportunity to exercise saving faith and accept Jesus Christ. . . .
6. At the great final judgement, all humans will be separated on the basis of their relationship to Christ during this life. Those who have believed in him will spend eternity in heaven. . . . Those who have not accepted him will experience hell, a place of unending suffering.[116]

Some of these points have been challenged by inclusivists, and others reinterpreted. While the necessity of belief (no. 3) was not necessarily rejected, its meaning has been broadened. The lostness of adherents of other religions (no. 4) has been challenged, and the end of the opportunity for faith (no. 5) has been disputed for a long time.

In a debate on salvation where they represent an evidentialist form of Christian particularism on salvation, Douglas Geivett and Gary Phillips call their position an "exclusivism or restrictivism" that insists on "explicit personal faith in Jesus Christ" for salvation; they identify their position as a narrower version of "Christian particularism."[117] For biblical evidence, they claim John 3:16, 18; 14:6; 17:20; Acts 4:12; and Romans 10:9–15.[118] A "biblical defense" is a standard tool for this position. In a three-way debate among representatives of restrictivism (Ronald Nash), inclusivism (John Sanders), and postmortem evangelization or divine perseverance (Gabriel Fackre), Ronald Nash also makes a strong biblical defense,[119] though his defense is as much an interpretation as others.

Universal Salvation

Proponents of universal salvation have different ideas about how everyone will be saved. Tom Greggs identifies two types of contemporary Christian universalism as "pluralistic universalism" and

116. Millard J. Erickson, "The State of the Question," in Crockett and Sigountos, *Through No Fault*, 23–24.
117. R. Douglas Geivett and W. Gary Phillips, "A Particularist View: An Evidentialist Approach," in Okholm and Phillips, *Four Views on Salvation*, 214.
118. Geivett and Phillips, "Particularist View," 230–37.
119. Ronald H. Nash, "Restrictivism," in Sanders, *What about Those Who Have Never Heard?*, 113–34.

"particularistic 'Christian' universalism."[120] David Bentley Hart, an Eastern Orthodox theologian, makes a historical-biblical argument for universalism based on God's absolute goodness.[121] Unlike Hart, who confidently articulates his firm conviction of universal salvation by dismissing the hell of eternal torment that often accompanies the Christian concept of salvation, Karl Barth leaves universal salvation as a "possibility." Interpreting salvation strictly in the light of God's revelation in Jesus Christ, Barth insists on "openness to the possibility that in the reality of God and man in Jesus Christ . . . there might be contained the super-abundant promise of the final deliverance of all men."[122] Following Barth closely, William Willimon puts the probability above a possibility when he says, "So even though it may be possible that many will be eternally damned, it's hard to square that with the Bible's depiction of a God who searches 'until' he finds."[123] Ironically, while Barth could not give up the possibility of universal salvation, Paul Knitter presents Barth as an exemplar of "total replacement"[124] theory for his insistence on salvation only through Christ as the revelation of God.

One line of argument for universalism or universal opportunity comes by way of biblical argument for postmortem evangelism. Salvation, according to postmortem evangelism, may be received either during one's lifetime or after death, and the argument has largely been based on Christ's preaching to "the spirits in prison" (1 Pet. 3:19) and "even to the dead" (4:6). The point seems to be that if you had no opportunity to hear the gospel during your lifetime, you will be given that opportunity after death. While a believer in postmortem evangelism can be a universalist (believing all must be saved), the argument may also end only in universal opportunity for salvation (all are given the opportunity to know and believe Christ as their savior).

---

120. Tom Greggs, "Christian Universalist View," in Johnson, *Five Views*, 197–98.
121. David Bentley Hart, *That All Shall Be Saved: Heaven, Hell, and Universal Salvation* (New Haven: Yale University Press, 2019).
122. Karl Barth, *Church Dogmatics* IV/3.1 (Edinburgh: T&T Clark, 1975), 477–78, quoted in Keith L. Johnson, *The Essential Karl Barth: A Reader and Commentary* (Grand Rapids: Baker Academic, 2019), 288–89.
123. William H. Willimon, *Who Will Be Saved?* (Nashville: Abingdon, 2008), 88.
124. Knitter, *Introducing Theologies of Religions*, 23–26.

Proponents of universal accessibility of salvation may fit more into the inclusivist category.

Gabriel Fackre uses the term "divine perseverance" for postmortem evangelization saying, "God is resolute, never giving up on getting the Word out . . . [even] to those we can't reach [in this world], even if it takes eternity."[125] He makes a case for postmortem evangelism with a theological argument based especially on theodicy and also on biblical exegesis of 1 Peter, Ephesians 4:8–9, and John 5:25.[126]

In Jathanna's study of the various proposals regarding the salvation of the unevangelized, particularly those born before the birth of Christ, he outlines seven thoughts before proposing his rebirth (reincarnation) theory. Three of the seven are on postmortem opportunities—that is, opportunity to receive Christ after death: (1) "Christ's preaching to the dead," based on 1 Peter 3:19 and 4:6; (2) "the Last Judgement as the time and place of the offer of salvation for the unevangelized"; and (3) "the Last Judgement on the basis of one's deeds of love towards the needy," based on Matthew 25:31–46.[127] The variety of postmortem receptions of the gospel of Christ put forward by scholars testifies to the different conceptual possibilities. They support the idea of universal salvation, especially for those who have no chance to hear the gospel during their lifetime.

Inclusive Soteriology

The position commonly called inclusivism is primarily a middle-of-the-road position. However, even this position is of varieties. A theology of fulfillment, popular among British Protestant missionaries working with Hindus and Buddhists in the late nineteenth and early twentieth centuries[128] and expressed most clearly by J. N. Farquhar in his 1913 book,[129] was an early version of the position.

125. Fackre, "Divine Perseverance," 73.
126. Fackre, "Divine Perseverance," 77–87.
127. Jathanna, *Decisiveness of the Christ-Event*, 437–46.
128. See Paul Hedges, *Preparation and Fulfillment: A History and Study of Fulfillment Theology in Modern British Thought in the Indian Context* (Bern, Switzerland: Peter Lang, 2001).
129. J. N. Farquhar, *The Crown of Hinduism* (London: Oxford University Press, 1913).

The theory sees Christ as the fulfillment of the religious and spiritual visions of other faiths. Paul Knitter uses the expression "Fulfillment Model" to refine what he earlier called the "Catholic Model" and deals almost exclusively with Catholic theology after Vatican II, including the theology of Karl Rahner.[130] Knitter's fulfillment model seems broader in reference and more nuanced than the British Protestants' theory of the early twentieth century. We have described evangelical inclusivism, which has a long history dating back as early as John Wesley. Suffice it to quote Clark Pinnock, who defines "cautious inclusivism" by saying, "Because God is present in the whole world (premise), God's grace is also at work in some ways among all people, possibly even in the sphere of religious life (inference). It entertains the possibility that religion may play a role in the salvation of the human race, a role preparatory to the gospel of Christ, in whom alone fullness of salvation is found."[131] The "less cautious" and "most famous inclusivist," according to Pinnock, is Karl Rahner,[132] whose name has been associated with the now famous "anonymous Christianity" theory in connection with salvation in other (non-Christian) religions.

The main conclusion of Rahner is that religions such as Hinduism, Buddhism, Indigenous religions, and others can be "ways of salvation,"[133] and their adherents can be anonymous Christians. To this end, Rahner put forth four theses. First, "Christianity understands itself as *the absolute religion*, intended for all men, which cannot recognize any other religion beside itself as of equal right."[134] It is on this seemingly arrogant thesis that Rahner's second and stunning thesis rested: "Until the moment when the gospel really enters into the historical situation of an individual, a non-Christian religion (even outside the Mosaic religion) does not merely contain elements of a natural knowledge of God. . . . It *contains also supernatural elements*

130. Knitter, *Introducing Theologies of Religions*, 63–103.
131. Clark H. Pinnock, "An Inclusivist View," in Okholm and Phillips, *Four Views on Salvation*, 98.
132. Pinnock, "Inclusivist View," 99.
133. Karl Rahner, *Foundations of Christian Faith* (New York: Crossroad, 1978), quoted in Knitter, *Introducing Theologies of Religions*, 71.
134. Karl Rahner, *Theological Investigations*, vol. 5, *Later Writings*, trans. Karl H. Kruger (Baltimore: Helicon, 1966), 118 (emphasis mine).

arising out of the grace which is given to men as a gratuitous gift on account of Christ."[135] This thesis strongly assumes God's will to save all human beings, which Rahner tries to reconcile with the first thesis—namely, the absoluteness of Christ as the savior of the world. Thus, he argues that "if, on the one hand, we conceive that salvation is specifically Christian, if there is no salvation apart from Christ . . . ; and if, on the other hand, God has really, truly and seriously intended this salvation for all men—then these two aspects cannot be reconciled in any other way than by stating that every human being is really and truly exposed to the influence of divine, supernatural grace which offers an interior union with God."[136] Thus, such a supernatural grace cannot but be located in the non-Christian (and pre-Christian) religions. The third thesis hangs entirely on the second: "If the second thesis is correct, then Christianity does not simply confront *the member of an extra-Christian religion as a mere non-Christian but as someone who can and must already be regarded in this or that respect as an anonymous Christian.*"[137] The fourth and final thesis directs Christians to regard "non-Christianity as Christianity of an anonymous kind" and "*go out to meet as a missionary, seeing it as a world which is to be brought to the explicit consciousness of what already belongs to it.*"[138] Rahner concludes, "Then, the Church will not so much regard herself today as the exclusive community of those who have a claim to salvation but rather as the historically tangible vanguard and the historically and socially constituted explicit expression of what the Christian hopes is present as a hidden reality even outside the visible Church."[139]

The varying viewpoints on the extent of God's salvation in Christ may best be understood by locating them on a spectrum between the universality of God's salvific will at one end and the particularity of redemption in Christ at the other end. The locations of the various viewpoints outlined above are based on their proximity from these two extreme positions.

135. Rahner, *Theological Investigations*, 121 (emphasis mine).
136. Rahner, *Theological Investigations*, 123.
137. Rahner, *Theological Investigations*, 131 (emphasis mine).
138. Rahner, *Theological Investigations*, 133 (emphasis original).
139. Rahner, *Theological Investigations*, 133.

An Inconclusive Conclusion: A Hermeneutical Observation

To conclude this discussion of the scope of salvation in contemporary thought, let me offer one final observation related to hermeneutics and what we may call the inconclusiveness of the matter. The particularity of Jesus's work of salvation and God's will to save all are the two points any reasonable interpretation must hold together consciously. The various positions we discussed can be located between these two theological points in such a way that their proximity to either of the two determines their theological locations. Interpreters who prioritize the sole saviorhood of Jesus can quickly reduce the universal saving will of God and explain it away as they restrict salvation to the explicit pronouncement of the name of Jesus. Similarly, those who emphasize God's universal salvation tend to either disparage the name and role of Jesus in God's saving act or make too general a point without attending to available details. Overemphasis on one at the expense of the other sacrifices interpretive credibility. Can we be so definitive about either of them or anything in between? Whether it is Karl Rahner's anonymous Christianity or Gaveitt and Phillips's appeal to scriptural evidence, when the entire Bible is taken together in the context of Christian tradition, any particular definitiveness melts.

"If you confess with your lips that Jesus is Lord and believe in your heart that God raised him from the dead, you will be saved" (Rom. 10:9). This is one of the most definite and explicit statements on the need for faith and confession for salvation. Yet when one considers this statement in its original (historical) context, where Jesus is unknown or simply not understood, the meanings of "believe" and "confess" are quite complicated. As he continues the letter, Paul asks, "How are they to believe in one of whom they have never heard?" (10:14). He responds by quoting Psalm 19:4: "Their voice has gone out to all the earth, and their words to the ends of the world" (Rom. 10:18). Whose voice and whose words are these? These are the voices and words of "the heavens" and "the firmament" (Ps. 19:1). In other words, they are the voices of creation. Earlier in the letter, Paul mentions revelation through the created order (Rom. 1:19–20), saying there can be no excuse for not knowing God revealed in creation. In other words, the good news of God's salvation in Christ is made known through the revelation in creation. Thus, one can confess the lordship of Jesus and his salvation through the knowledge of God revealed in the created order. N. T. Wright objects to this seemingly clear reference on the grounds that "if the message were so effectively proclaimed by creation itself, the need for apostles, carefully set out in vv. 14–17, would be undermined."[140] Wright's claim is blatantly implausible. For one, it rests on what he determines is effective. Secondly, it is unlikely that Paul would quote the Scripture in such a twisted way to mean something other than what the quoted text meant. Thus, as far as Romans 10 is concerned, it is reasonable to believe that God's words conveyed through the voice of creation are enough to convey God's saving knowledge in Christ Jesus. Could those who have never explicitly heard the name of Jesus have heard of him and his salvation? Is it possible, according to this passage? It seems so!

In this light, Karl Barth's way of being open to the "possibility" of universal salvation makes sense. It is a possibility, but the definitive answer belongs to God. While firm in his belief that Christ is the savior, "Barth refused to lock God into either an 'All are saved' or 'Not all are saved' position."[141] Lesslie Newbigin forcefully argues that Christian theologians and leaders should not pretend to know who will be saved and who will not be saved. Drawing general principles from the New Testament teaching, Newbigin observes that the "emphasis is always on surprise. It is the sinners who will be welcomed and those who are confident that their place was secure who will find themselves outside. God will shock the righteous by his limitless generosity and by his tremendous severity."[142] Along the same lines, Willimon asserts that "only God knows our final destiny. This is not a cause for discouragement or paralyzing insecurity. It is a basis of our faith."[143] This is how the ecumenical discussion during the 1970s and 1980s in the World Council of Churches concluded the heated debate about Christians and people of other faiths. The World Mission and Evangelism Conference of 1989 in San Antonio,

---

140. Wright, "Letter to the Romans," 10:668.

141. Willimon, *Who Will Be Saved?*, 75.

142. Lesslie Newbigin, *The Open Secret: An Introduction to the Theology of Mission*, rev. ed. (Grand Rapids: Eerdmans, 1995), 173.

143. Willimon, *Who Will Be Saved?*, 89.

Texas, showed a posture of significant humility in its statement; while affirming that "Christians owe the message of God's salvation in Jesus Christ to every person and to every people" in its "evangelistic mandate," it emphatically states that "we may never claim to have a full understanding of God's truth: we are only recipients of God's grace."[144] When it comes to the salvation of Christ in relation to other religions, it says, "We cannot point to any other way of salvation than Jesus Christ; at the same time we cannot set limits to the saving power of God."[145] While the significance of the statement was not recognized immediately, in historical hindsight, the statement of San Antonio on "Witness among People of Other Living Faiths" came to be recognized as momentous. In its "History of World Mission and Evangelism," the World Council of Churches' website describes it as a "remarkable . . . consensus statement reached on the relation between Christianity and other religions."[146]

144. Fredrick R. Wilson, ed., *The San Antonio Report: Your Will be Done; Mission in Christ's Way* (Geneva: World Council of Churches, 1990), 32.
145. Wilson, *San Antonio Report*, 32.
146. World Council of Churches, "Commission on World Mission and Evangelism: History," accessed September 24, 2021, https://archived.oikoumene.org/en/what-we-do/cwme/history.

4

THE LIVING CHURCH IN GOD'S MISSION

Theological Consideration of the Church in History

Somewhat emulating Augustine's famous description of the church as a "mixed body of saints and sinners" (*corpus mixtum*),[1] Wallace Alston Jr. makes an illuminating point on the basic nature of the church in his book *The Church of the Living God*. He writes, "The church of Jesus Christ is a strange affair, a mixed bag we might say today. . . . On the one hand, the church is an organization, and institution, a form of association like any other. On the other hand, if we are to believe the things often said about it, the church is completely different, without analogy or parallel, absolutely unique."[2] As a part of our effort to trace the theological dimension of Christian faith and God's mission in the world, our concern is on the latter—namely, the theology and uniqueness of the church. This is not to divorce

---

1. For an extract of Augustine's argument, see "Augustine on the Mixed Nature of the Church," in *The Christian Theology Reader*, ed. Alister E. McGrath, 3rd ed. (Oxford: Blackwell, 2007), 496–97.
2. Wallace Alston Jr., *The Church of the Living God: A Reformed Perspective* (Louisville: Westminster John Knox, 2002), 1.

theology from reality, but quite the opposite, to direct the church in the real world to its authentic identity as "the church of the living God," even if such authenticity remains idealistic.

Robert Jenson rightly differentiates two major perspectives on the theological study of the church. He says, "Whether we are to say that God uses the gospel to gather the church for himself, or that God provides the church to carry the gospel to the world, depends entirely on the direction of thoughts in a context."[3] Treating the church from a systematic theological viewpoint, Jenson opts for the former. Our direction of thought is certainly the latter, while holding that the two thoughts cannot really be separated. As Daniel Migliore astutely states, "God enters into covenant with creatures and seeks their partnership. If there is communion in the eternal life of God and God wills us to share in that communion, then questions regarding the nature of the church and its mission in the world today, far from being matters of secondary importance to the Christian faith, are quite central."[4]

Despite the fact that the doctrine of the church did not feature widely in early theological debates, it secured an important place in the Nicene Creed. The Nicene statement of the church as "one, holy, catholic, and apostolic" remains authoritative, and today most historic Christian traditions regard these as attributes of the true church.[5] Until the church occupied a significant place in society under Emperor Constantine in the fourth century, its theological identity was not a major issue. When the church held ecumenical councils to clarify its beliefs, it did so with an assumed authority. The first significant theological debate resulting in due consideration of the church came from Augustine, who made strong theological arguments regarding the life of the church as he dealt with the Donatist controversy. Despite criticism by some today that Augustine's ecclesiology was Neoplatonic, his rich contribution

3. Robert Jenson, *Systematic Theology*, vol. 2, *The Works of God* (New York: Oxford University Press, 1999), 168.

4. Daniel L. Migliore, *Faith Seeking Understanding: An Introduction to Christian Theology*, 2nd ed. (Grand Rapids: Eerdmans, 2004), 248–49.

5. Alston, *Church of the Living God*, 52; Avery Dulles, *Models of the Church*, exp. ed. (New York: Doubleday, 2002), 118–20.

earned him recognition as the "Doctor of Ecclesiology."[6] The Reformation featured the next serious theological debate, and post-Reformation polemics between the competing claims of Catholics and Protestants to be the true church of God influenced much theological consideration until the dawning of the ecumenical age in the twentieth century. This ecumenical fervor seems to have yielded strong interest in the theology of the church, such that the twentieth century produced more theological studies of the church than any other period in history.[7]

With this deserved attention, the church has been studied in different ways and from different viewpoints. From sociological studies of congregations and empirical analyses of church life, social scientists have helped to paint realistic pictures of church life.[8] Beyond studying congregations as they exist, others have identified the potential of congregational public witness as a way of witnessing to God's mission in the world.[9] Yet even when the church is cast as a human association like any other organization, the distinctive mark of the church is its uniqueness as a community of faith. The new interest in ecclesiology has largely been at the front of theological studies, and the contribution of thinkers imprecisely labeled "social Trinitarians" is significant.[10] Works of well-known scholars, such as Jürgen Moltmann and Wolfhart Pannenberg within Protestant ecumenical church traditions, John Zizioulas in the Orthodox tradition, and post-Vatican-II Catholic scholars Joseph Ratzinger and Hans Küng,

---

6. James K. Lee, *Augustine and the Mystery of the Church* (Minneapolis: Fortress, 2017), xv.

7. In Robert Jenson's words, "It is only in this [twentieth] century and most decisively in its ecumenical efforts that the church has come to see herself as a theological question." Prior to this period, he says, "she has understood herself as a presupposition of theology." Jenson, *Systematic Theology*, 2:168.

8. For a good guideline, see Nancy T. Ammerman et al., eds., *Studying Congregations: A New Handbook* (Nashville: Abingdon, 1998).

9. Gregg Okesson, for instance, deftly proposes congregational witness to the triune God in the public spaces as a "public missiology." See Gregg Okesson, *A Public Missiology: How Local Churches Witness to a Complex World* (Grand Rapids: Baker Academic, 2020).

10. See, e.g., Gijsbert van den Brink, "Social Trinitarianism: A Discussion of Some Recent Theological Criticisms," *International Journal of Systematic Theology* 16, no. 3 (July 2014): 331–50.

have been followed by a host of other scholarly engagements.[11] Moltmann's appeal to move away from passive church membership to
active engagement with and in the church, for instance, sparked
new interests, while Hans Küng's call for constant renewal of the
church to assume anew its responsibility has inspired new genera-
tions of thinkers.

Together with Moltmann's works,[12] Pannenberg's insistence on
the theological universality of the church in the eschaton[13] helped
establish the missionary theology of the church in the world. Out
of the mid-twentieth-century ecumenical quest for the theological
foundation of the church's mission, the significance of the church's
universality or catholicity as its missional foundation became clear.
Connecting new ecclesiological interest with trinitarian renaissance
is an ongoing development, as we see in the works of scholars like
Miroslav Volf and Robert Sherman. Also quite significant is the new
interest shown by evangelical theologians and their contributions
in the discussion.[14] In this chapter we attempt to look at the church
holistically as God's mission to the world. The church has no reason
to exist outside God's mission in the world.

From Schismatic Groupings to Mutual Engagement: A Historical Recollection of Ecumenical Ecclesiology

Before we deal with major biblical images and themes surrounding
the church in the mission of God, we will trace a few lines of historical

11. For an introduction to the works of some of these theologians of ecclesiological renewal, see Veli-Matti Kärkkäinen, *An Introduction to Ecclesiology: Ecumenical,
Historical & Global Perspectives* (Downers Grove, IL: IVP Academic, 2002), 95–165.

12. Jürgen Moltmann, *The Church in the Power of the Spirit: A Contribution
to Messianic Ecclesiology* (New York: Harper & Row, 1977). Moltmann recognizes
the theology of mission as "one of the strongest impulses towards the renewal of the
theological concept of the church" today (p. 7).

13. Wolfhart Pannenberg, *The Church*, trans. Keith Crim (Philadelphia: Westminster, 1983), see esp. 44–68.

14. See, e.g., John G. Stackhouse Jr., ed., *Evangelical Ecclesiology: Reality or Illu-
sion?* (Grand Rapids: Baker Academic, 2003); Brad Harper and Paul Louis Metzger,
Exploring Ecclesiology: An Evangelical and Ecumenical Introduction (Grand Rapids:
Brazos, 2009); Mark Husbands and Daniel J. Treier, eds., *The Community of the
Word: Toward an Evangelical Ecclesiology* (Downers Grove, IL: InterVarsity, 2005).

development in contemporary ecclesiological renewal. Because the church is a faith community whose basis and central tenets were established some twenty centuries ago and its historical experience is the strength of its own life, this study is paramount. While most studies of the history of the church have focused on dominant traditions and confessional bodies, the internationalization of knowledge since the last quarter of the twentieth century affords us a more comprehensive and ecumenical (or interconfessional) approach. In fact, no isolated denominational study can really be done today without reference to other denominations or traditions. In his global-ecumenical introduction to the church, Veli-Matti Kärkkäinen lines up the ecclesiologies of different confessional traditions quite neatly.[15] Our goal in this chapter is to find an ecclesiological self-understanding in God's mission in which we identify the missionary call of the church. This can be done, we believe, only in the ecumenical context of the church.

The twentieth century saw revolutionary changes in the church's thinking and practice. Such changes came in large part from the mutual interactions among churches of different traditions. The Protestant-led modern ecumenical movement helped to upend the divisive conception of the church and initiated a significant movement toward unity among Protestants and, later, the Orthodox churches. The most significant transformation of the concept of church in Roman Catholicism came through Vatican II, and its impact was felt in other churches. Cooperation and mutual engagement among historic confessional bodies and a collaborative spirit swept even independent churches. From their monolithic, denominationally isolated, and combative past,[16] most churches had become relatively open and respectful of each other by the end of the twentieth century. The self-understanding of churches changed as they sought deeper meanings of their call.

15. Kärkkäinen, *Introduction to Ecclesiology*, 17–91.
16. Much of the history of ecumenism to the end of the nineteenth century was either within confessions (confessional alliances) or in a few marginal cooperations outside the church. See the chapters by Martin Schmidt, Norman Sykes, George Florovsky, Don Herbert Yoder, and Henry Renaud Turner Brandreth in Ruth Rouse and Stephen C. Neill, eds., *A History of the Ecumenical Movement*, vol. 1, *1517–1948*, 4th ed. (Geneva: World Council of Churches, 1993), 73–306.

Among Protestants, cooperation became the key component and
the agent of change. Although the Protestant missionary movement
began as a voluntary society mostly outside the structure of the
church, by the beginning of the twentieth century it had become
the most powerful uniting force for the church. From its beginning
at the margins of the church, the modern missionary movement became the mother of the modern ecumenical church. Collaborations
in the mission field brought missionaries together for the sharing of
ideas and experiences and eventually led to cooperative conferences.[17]
From conferences in the mission field, the movement reached back to
the home church. The decadal missionary cooperative conferences
among Euro-American missionary societies climaxed in the now famous World Missionary Conference of Edinburgh in 1910.[18] As "the
birthplace of the modern ecumenical movement,"[19] Edinburgh 1910
helped to change Protestant ecclesiology for good. Two independent
movements inspired by the conference, the Faith and Order Movement[20] and the Life and Work Movement,[21] joined together to form
the WCC, which was officially inaugurated on August 23, 1948, in
its First Assembly in Amsterdam.[22]

From a narrow parochial denominationalism, Protestant churches
developed an organic, ecumenical spirit. This new atmosphere was
conducive to ecclesiological renewal as interest grew discernibly.
Kärkkäinen rightly observes that "the main catalyst for the rapidly
growing ecclesiological interest has been the ecumenical movement.

17. See William Richey Hogg, *Ecumenical Foundations: A History of the Inter-*
national Missionary Council and Its Nineteenth-Century Background (New York:
Harper & Brothers, 1952), 15–34. For the earliest period of Protestant missionary
cooperation, see R. Pierce Beaver, *Ecumenical Beginnings in Protestant World Mis-*
sion: A History of Comity (New York: Thomas Nelson & Sons, 1962).
18. Hogg, *Ecumenical Foundations*, 35–142.
19. Kenneth Scott Latourette, "Ecumenical Bearings of the Missionary Movement and the International Missionary Council," in Rouse and Neill, *History of the*
Ecumenical Movement, 362.
20. See Tissington Tatlow, "The World Conference on Faith and Order," in Rouse
and Neill, *History of the Ecumenical Movement*, 405–41.
21. Nils Ehrenström, "Movements for International Fellowship and Life and Work,
1925–1948," in Rouse and Neill, *History of the Ecumenical Movement*, 545–96.
22. Willem Adolf Visser 't Hooft, "The Genesis of the World Council of Churches,"
in Rouse and Neill, *History of the Ecumenical Movement*, 720.

No other movement in the history of the Christian church, perhaps with the exception of the Reformation, has shaped the thinking and practice of Christendom as much as the modern movement for Christian unity."[23] The dwindling of the WCC's influence and its declining role in the global theological conversations are undeniable, but amid various misunderstandings within and without, the WCC achieved its goal and even outlived its raison d'être as "a fellowship of churches."[24]

There were historical moments when the WCC may have played a role more divisive than unitive. This was especially so in the 1960s when evangelical Christians became very uncomfortable with what they considered to be humanistic and liberal theology's domination of the WCC.[25] Evangelical Christians rallied against the WCC, eventually forming a separate movement, which came to be called the Lausanne Congress for World Evangelization. At its height, the tension was centered on works versus words, or social action versus proclamation of the gospel. Through the influence of moderates and especially through the emergence of in-depth evangelical theology, we have been seeing a growing ecumenical spirit of mutuality. The evangelicals' embrace of a "holistic mission" that integrates word and deed, something similar to what was seen at the integration of Life and Work with Faith and Order movements to form the WCC in the 1930s, led to openness on the evangelical side. Meanwhile, the decline of radicalism for a more inclusive spirit in the WCC also decreased the tension.

What is most significant in terms of the ecumenical character of the WCC is the participation of the Orthodox churches, both Eastern (Chalcedonian) and Oriental (non-Chalcedonian) churches. Eastern

23. Kärkkäinen, *Introduction to Ecclesiology*, 7–8.

24. "Constitution and Rules of the World Council of Churches" (as amended by the Central Committee of the WCC, Geneva, Switzerland, 2018), accessed September 25, 2021, https://www.oikoumene.org/resources/documents/constitution-and-rules -of-the-world-council-of-churches.

25. Evident in influential American evangelical voices such as Billy Graham and church-growth proponent Donald A. McGavran. See Graham, "Why the Berlin Congress?," *Christianity Today* 11, no. 3 (November 11, 1966): 3–7; McGavran, "Will Uppsala Betray the Two Billion?," *Church Growth Bulletin*, May 1968, reproduced in *The Eye of the Storm: The Great Debate in Mission*, ed. Donald A. McGavran (Waco: Word, 1972), 233–41.

Orthodox churches began to participate meaningfully and actively
in the movement as early as the 1920s. In fact, one of the earliest and
most significant calls for unity in the history of the ecumenical movement was issued by the Ecumenical Patriarch of Constantinople in a
1920 encyclical entitled "Unto the Churches of Christ Everywhere."[26]
In a passionate plea based on the biblical call to love one another,
the encyclical appeals for "league (fellowship) between churches."[27]
Yet political circumstances kept many of the Eastern churches from
the WCC when it was inaugurated in 1948.[28] At a consultation in
Moscow just a month before the WCC's inauguration, representatives
of Orthodox churches "decided to refrain from participation in the
ecumenical movement" as it was then constituted,[29] only to join the
council in the Third Assembly in New Delhi in 1961. It is ironic that
most of the Orthodox churches joined the WCC at the same time
as when the first of the Pentecostal churches joined the WCC in the
New Delhi assembly.

Orthodox membership in the WCC and its participation in wider
ecumenical developments have brought benefits to the Christian
world in various ways, enriching doctrinal conversations in general
and helping to change and enlarge theological views on key concepts.
The influences are most noticeable in the trinitarian conception of the
church and its mission. Although the Orthodox tradition did not have
a direct role in the rise of the *missio Dei* conception within the WCC
in the mid-twentieth century, its strong presence in the ecumenical
movement from the early 1960s helped to shape the conversation.
The emerging trinitarian ecclesiology also owes much to Orthodox
theology and missions.

26. "Unto the Churches of Christ Everywhere: Encyclical of the Ecumenical
Patriarchate, 1920," in *The Ecumenical Movement: An Anthology of Key Texts
and Voices*, ed. Michael Kinnamon and Brian E. Cope (Grand Rapids: Eerdmans,
1997), 11–14.

27. "Unto the Churches of Christ," 13.

28. Vasil T. Istavridis, "The Orthodox Churches in the Ecumenical Movement,
1948–1968," in *The Ecumenical Advance: A History of the Ecumenical Movement*,
vol. 2, *1948–1968*, ed. Harold E. Fey, 3rd ed. (Geneva: World Council of Churches,
1993), 305.

29. Nicolas Zernov, "The Eastern Churches and the Ecumenical Movement in
the Twentieth Century," in Rouse and Neill, *History of the Ecumenical Movement*,
667.

In its ecclesiology, the Catholic Church was transformed almost wholly in and by the Vatican II Council (1962–65). The process of transformation captured in its keyword *aggiornamento* (updating or renewing) began when Pope John XXIII revealed the plan of the council. Two of the four core constitutional documents produced by the council are directly about the church: the Dogmatic Constitution of the Church (*Lumen Gentium*)[30] and the Pastoral Constitution of the Church in the Modern World (*Gaudium et Spes*).[31] In his theological commentary on the council, Joseph Ratzinger (later Pope Benedict XVI) describes "the debate of the Church" in the second session as the real beginning of the work of the council.[32] More than anything, the council transformed the concept of the church as exemplified by the contrast between the old (rejected) text and the new (adopted) text of *Lumen Gentium*. Avery Dulles highlights the contrast by noting the title of the first chapter, which changed from "The Nature of the Church Militant" to "The Mystery of the Church." He calls this change of titles "symptomatic of the whole ecclesiology of the Council."[33] The text of the "Constitution of the Church" became the theological foundation of the council's conception of the church. This text, Ratzinger affirms, "returned wholeheartedly to the total biblical testimony about the Church."[34] What captured the shift most significantly in the Catholic Church's self-conception in relation to the universal "Church of Christ" is expressed in a single phrase in *Lumen Gentium*, which says, "This Church [of Christ], constituted and organized in the world as a society, subsists in the Catholic Church." The term "subsists in" replaces "is" of the previous draft

30. For the complete text of the constitution, see "*Lumen Gentium*: Dogmatic Constitution on the Church Solemnly Promulgated by His Holiness Pope Paul VI on November 21, 1964," Vatican, accessed July 23, 2020, http://www.vatican.va /archive/hist_councils/ii_vatican_council/documents/vat-ii_const_19641121_lumen -gentium_en.html.

31. See "*Gaudium et spes*: Pastoral Constitution on the Church in the Modern World Promulgated by His Holiness, Pope Paul VI on December 7, 1965," Vatican, accessed July 23, 2020, http://www.vatican.va/archive/hist_councils/ii_vatican_council /documents/vat-ii_const_19651207_gaudium-et-spes_en.html.

32. Joseph Ratzinger, *Theological Highlights of Vatican II* (New York: Paulist Press, 2009), 71–90.

33. Dulles, *Models of the Church*, 9.

34. Ratzinger, *Theological Highlights*, 74.

and became "one of the most significant steps taken by Vatican II," says Dulles.[35] The move is from claiming itself to be the church of Christ to identifying itself as a part of the church of Christ.

In his influential book *Models of the Church*, Dulles traces the historical developments that led to Vatican II and offers some post-conciliar thoughts. After a long period of the stable model of the church as "institution," which culminated around Vatican I (1869–70), Vatican II brought a new paradigm followed by rapid changes of paradigms. Although the historical developments he describes in Catholic ecclesiology can be a bit confusing for non-Catholics, his theological observations on the church explicate the new ecclesiology neatly. He sees changes from "Mystical Body" to "People of God, Sacrament, and Servant" as paradigmatic shifts.[36] Perhaps what he sees as rapid changes of ecclesiastical paradigms are just further developments of the one new paradigm. At any rate, the four new models from and after Vatican II that he explores—communion, sacrament, herald, and servant—powerfully represent the Catholic Church's current ecclesiology.

One of the most significant recognitions of the church's identity in the twentieth century was that of its missionary character as shown by different confessional traditions and denominations. Built on the new and theologically vital understanding of the church in *Lumen Gentium*, Vatican II's decree on the "Missionary Activity of the Church" (*Ad Gentes*) is well grounded in ecclesiology. The decree begins with its principal statement: "The pilgrim Church is missionary by its very nature, since it is from the mission of the Son and the mission of the Holy Spirit that she draws her origin, in accordance with the decree of God the Father."[37] In other words, the church's trinitarian origin has made it missionary in its very being. The strength of *Ad Gentes* is its integration of the theology of the church (*Lumen Gentium*) with the missionary calling. Such important themes as sacrament, catholicity, and apostolicity are integrated in

35. Dulles, *Models of the Church*, 117.
36. Dulles, *Models of the Church*, 22.
37. For the text of the decree, see "*Ad gentes*: Decree on the Mission Activity of the Church," Vatican, accessed September 18, 2020, http://www.vatican.va/archive/hist _councils/ii_vatican_council/documents/vat-ii_decree_19651207_ad-gentes_en.html.

the trinitarian theology with specific missionary callings, such as evangelization and church planting.

In Protestant-driven ecumenical discussions, the reconception of mission as *missio Dei* from the 1950s continued to reverberate. After a lull following polarized interpretations of a world-centered understanding (progressive liberals) and a church-centered understanding of the *missio Dei*, the concept of mission took a new ecclesiastical turn and was revived at the turn of the twenty-first century in North America. Its application is seen in the name "missional church" or "missional ecclesiology." Greatly influenced by Protestant missionary Lesslie Newbigin, this new theologically informed and contextually driven ecclesiology gained traction in Western churches within a short period. Newbigin, a longtime missionary bishop in South India and an ecumenical leader, challenged Western churches to a new missionary engagement with their own post-Enlightenment culture.[38] Early proponents saw their efforts as a way of taking up "the Newbigin gauntlet"[39] for domestic missiology in the West, and the idea of missional church came about as a result of concerted reflections by a networking group that followed Newbigin, especially his call for "a genuine encounter between the gospel and our [Western] culture."[40] The group, which fittingly called itself The Gospel and Our Culture Network,[41] introduced the term "missional" as an essential theological qualifier of the church in this new missionary calling. Quite similar to Vatican II's conception of the church as missionary by its very nature, the Network conceives of the church as primarily missionary by qualifying it as "missional." The case is built on the theology of *missio Dei* by defining "the church as God's instrument

38. First introduced in his book written for the British churches: Newbigin, *The Other Side of 1984: Questions for the Churches* (Geneva: World Council of Churches, 1983). The case is expanded and deepened in Lesslie Newbigin, *Foolishness to the Greek: The Gospel and Western Culture* (Grand Rapids: Eerdmans, 1986).

39. George R. Hunsberger, "The Newbigin Gauntlet: Developing a Domestic Missiology for North America," *Missiology: An International Review* 19, no. 4 (October 1991): 391–408.

40. Newbigin, *Foolishness to the Greek*, 43.

41. See Darrell L. Guder, ed., *Missional Church: A Vision for the Sending of the Church in North America* (Grand Rapids: Eerdmans, 1998), 3. Also see "What and Why," The Gospel and Our Culture Network, 2017, https://gocn.org/about-us/what -and-why/.

for God's mission"[42] and emphasizing it as "an alternative or contrast community." The church, therefore, "should focus on and arise out of the formation of particular communities of God's people, called and sent where they are as witnesses to the gospel."[43] Called to be God's witness, the church, therefore, *is* mission before it *does* mission.

The concept gained momentum quickly and with high velocity. The theological grounds laid by the pioneering proponents were explicated and expanded.[44] What this concept does well is connect a theological idea with an ecclesial practice that various churches and denominational bodies can adopt and adapt for themselves. As the interest spread, especially in churches, the interpretations and the translations in practice came to highlight some issues. One of the concept's major strengths is its emphasis on the church's call to its context or missions in the church's cultural location. But as a project of white Christian thinkers, its insistence on "our culture" makes it appear as just another Euro-American project, and this time exclusively for itself. That does not appear to be what the proponents intended, but in practice, the missional church came to assume such a position. While the idea closely resonates with how many non-Western Christians relate the church and missions, the close connection of the missional church with Western culture branded it an exclusively Western church project. Secondly, as Craig Ott and Stephen Strauss argue, the missional church's emphasis on the being rather than the doing of missions, together with its stress on local witness, has the potential to erode cross-cultural missionary practice.[45] This may be adding to the decline of intercultural and international missionary works on the part of the Western mainline churches. Yet despite these pitfalls, the missional church has uplifted the cause of mission theologically and practically and has brought a theologically grounded ecclesiology of mission.

42. Guder, *Missional Church*, 8.
43. Guder, *Missional Church*, 9.
44. For an early mapping of the expanding conversations, see Craig Van Gelder and Dwight J. Zscheile, *The Missional Church in Perspective: Mapping Trends and Shaping the Conversation* (Grand Rapids: Baker Academic, 2011), 67–98.
45. Craig Ott and Stephen J. Strauss with Timothy C. Tennent, *Encountering Theology of Mission: Biblical Foundations, Historical Developments, and Contemporary Issues* (Grand Rapids: Baker Academic, 2010), 200–201.

As indicated before, one benefit of the ecclesiastical renewal we are seeing today is the ecumenical spirit in which churches now exist. Despite the challenges of the secularizing world and the strong denominational feelings in some circles, Christians of different confessions and churches have come much closer to each other. Overall, the sense of mutuality and cooperation has grown among Christian communities. The impending globalization that forces people of different religions to coexist has also provided a conducive setting for cooperation and mutuality. Churches of different confessions and traditions have come to understand their differences and similarities in practical terms and to respect each other. Claiming to be *the* true church is largely frowned upon, though there is wide agreement on what makes *a* true church as each is striving to do better.

At the denominational and confessional level, churches hold dear their distinct confessions and unique identities—but not necessarily against each other, as in the past. What we read in history negatively as "schism" is now positively described as the birth-event of new traditions. At the intellectual level, there appears to be a general consensus as to what constitutes a good and "true" church. Whether a church is creed-oriented in its worship or not, the Nicaean-Constantinopolitan confession of the church as "one, holy, catholic, and apostolic" seems to constitute the marks of the true church most consensually. However, the understanding of these four marks varies greatly. Howard Snyder suggests that these marks can be ambiguous and prone to misuse, and they can be understood as representing only one-half of the church's story. A careful study of biblical ecclesiology, he says, reveals the "missing half." He creatively pairs the missing half with these traditional marks as follows: "The church is *many* as well as *one*"; "the church is *charismatic* as well as *holy*"; "the church is both *universal* and *local*"; and "the church is *prophetic* as well as *apostolic*."[46] No serious theologian of the Bible would deny these extensions as they show the dynamism of the church and the marks themselves.[47]

Studies on the missionary aspects of the church have tended to focus on the mark of apostolicity, the treatment of which, according

46. Howard Snyder, "The Marks of Evangelical Ecclesiology," in Stackhouse, *Evangelical Ecclesiology*, 85–88 (emphasis original).
47. Also see Moltmann, *Church in the Power of the Spirit*, 337–42.

to John Flett, is often skewed historically by the separation of "cultivation of the faith" as a spiritual matter and "communication of the faith" as a missionary matter.[48] Both Catholics and Protestants prioritize the former under the rubric of apostolic orthodoxy as seen in the debates on apostolic succession. The church's intent to faithfully hold the apostolic tradition often comes at the neglect of "cross-cultural engagement and appropriation of the gospel."[49] In other words, in its attempt to stay true to its faith, the church mostly decimates the communication of the faith aspect even in its understanding of apostolicity. The cultivation and the communication of the Christian faith should be given equal importance, and they should go hand in hand. Similarly, one of the marks of the church cannot be singled out meaningfully without considering the others. Although the "apostolic" nature marks the missionary character of the church most clearly, its significance and meanings must be derived in connection with the other marks.

Different confessional bodies achieve the marks of the true church in their own ways within their broader ecclesiastical traditions. Orthodox and Roman Catholic churches, which have kept these four marks of the church alive, largely understood them in a historical sense. Eastern Orthodox and Catholic churches claim themselves to be the organic continuation of the church (in the Chalcedonian tradition) while Oriental Orthodox churches make their own theological claim as against Chalcedonian tradition. Orthodox ecclesiology tends to emphasize the spiritual and practical aspects,[50] and Catholic ecclesiology has made quite a journey from institutional to theological. For churches of the Protestant Reformation, these four marks of the church develop from the right preaching and hearing of the gospel, and in the right administration of the sacraments according to the original intent.[51] Understanding and accepting each other in our differences for mutual coexistence and cooperation have now become the order of the day.

---

48. John G. Flett, *Apostolicity: The Ecumenical Question in World Christian Perspective* (Downers Grove, IL: IVP Academic, 2016), 16.
49. Flett, *Apostolicity*, 16.
50. Kärkkäinen, *Introduction to Ecclesiology*, 12–25.
51. Alston, *Church of the Living God*, 52.

Analogical Images and Theology of the Church

Avery Dulles says that theological realities are mysteries to a large extent, often best explained using analogies. As with other theological realities we have discussed, such as God and salvation, the Bible uses a variety of analogical images and metaphors to depict the meaning and purposes of the church. We will look into a few of these images and motifs to discern the theological identity and purpose of the church in the mission of God. We will first briefly discuss how these images and themes have been drawn together in recent studies and then outline what we believe to be the most significant images of the church that reflect God's mission in the world.

If Jesus's promise to build his church, which he entrusted with the authority to bind and loose (Matt. 16:18–19; 18:15–18), was fulfilled in the church community that came into being after Pentecost, then the church is not just a human organization; it is a people dedicated for the mission of God in Jesus. The church is the community of people whose faith in Jesus Christ as the promised Messiah of God and the savior of the world is its distinguishing mark. It is a community that believes in the one God of Israel, accepting Jesus of Nazareth as the Christ of God, through whose teachings and work (including his sacrificial death) the church receives God's eternal blessed life in the power of his Spirit and through whom it worships and serves God. As a community, it is centered on Jesus Christ as the way to God, and it commits itself to testify about him, believing that he is presently active in the church's life in and through the power of the Holy Spirit. To be a church or to belong to one is to declare faith in God through Jesus Christ in the power of the Holy Spirit.

The church, as a theological reality, is incredibly difficult to define, and thus, the Bible uses various analogical images. In what has become a classic in the study of the biblical theology of the church, Paul Minear enumerates the different images used in the New Testament and depicts major aspects of the church and its converging characteristics. He counts the images that refer, in one way or another, to the church and finds more than eighty.[52] Making a "rough

---

52. Paul S. Minear, *Images of the Church in the New Testament* (Louisville: Westminster John Knox, 2004), 28.

and tentative" classification, he categorizes these images into minor images[53] and major constellations, according to their basic functions.[54] The "three constellations" are (1) "images that gravitate around the conception of the church as the people of God," (2) those gravitating around God's creation of "a new humanity" (or the new creation), and (3) those gravitating around "the church as a fellowship of saints and slaves whose life together is characterized by a unique kind of mutuality in gift and in vocation."[55] Independent of these three gravitating themes, Minear deals separately with (4) the church as the body of Christ, as presented by Paul. Following Minear's method and argument, John Driver identifies biblical images of the church in missions under four major groups: (1) pilgrimage images, (2) new order images, (3) peoplehood images, and (4) images of transformation.[56] Significant are images that relate the church with salvation and conversion, such as the church as a new creation, as a new order, or as a transformed community. These are images of the church in connection with God's salvific work as we have discussed in previous chapters. To avoid redundancy, we will not deal with them again here, leaving us with two main images of the church: the people of God on a pilgrimage and a fellowshipping community in the body of Christ.

In what may be considered one of the best recent studies on the biblical theology of Christian mission, Stanley Skreslet skillfully employs five biblical images to depict the what and the how of mission in the Bible.[57] He begins by defining Christian mission as "acting in the name of Jesus Christ with the intention of communicating or demonstrating to others something substantive about the Good News that defines the believing fellowship of the church."[58] The strengths of this definition lie in its centering on the good news as the essence of the church and in its emphasis on action ("communicating" and "demonstrating"). Skreslet's selected images depict the missionary

53. Minear includes thirty-two images under this category and deals with each independently. Minear, *Images of the Church*, 28–65.
54. Minear, *Images of the Church*, 67.
55. Minear, *Images of the Church*, 67.
56. John Driver, *Images of the Church in Mission* (Scottsdale, PA: Herald, 1997).
57. Stanley H. Skreslet, *Picturing Christian Witness: New Testament Images of Disciples in Mission* (Grand Rapids: Eerdmans, 2006), 27.
58. Skreslet, *Picturing Christian Witness*, 27.

call of the disciples in the New Testament, with an emphasis on the gospel (or good news). When theology of mission is structured in a broader framework as the church's participation in God's missionary work, the scope of the images appears broader and their metaphorical meanings widened. However, any exclusion of the gospel's communication in the world from the church's missionary nature and call would miss an essential mark of the missionary church.

Drawing mainly from the historical experience of the Catholic Church, together with some thoughts from Protestant theologians, Avery Dulles outlines five basic models of the church. He provides a good theoretical passageway between images and models. He writes, "When an image is employed reflectively and critically to deepen one's theoretical understanding of a reality it becomes what is today called a 'model.'"[59] Thus, drawing from biblical images of the church in the historical experience of the church, he identifies the following models of the church:[60] (1) the church as institution, (2) the church as mystical communion, (3) the church as sacrament, (4) the church as herald, and (5) the church as servant. While the first model may be more of an existential (practical) necessity than a theological model, the other four are theological-spiritual models drawn from biblical teachings. The church as institution is a pre-Vatican-II driving concept in the Catholic Church, and its dominance ended with the council.

Dulles's "church as mystical communion" combines two central images that we have identified in the works of Minear and Driver— namely, the church as people of God and the body of Christ. Dulles convincingly distinguishes the communion model from the institution model using the German *Gesellschaft* (formally organized or structured society) and *Gemeinschaft* (informal or interpersonal community).[61] The shift from the former to the latter is clear in Vatican II, yet both constitute peoplehood of the church. Thus far our discussion of the works of Minear, Driver, and Dulles directs us to a few major images of the church, including the people of God, the body of Christ, and the fellowship of saints and sinners. In his

59. Dulles, *Models of the Church*, 15.
60. Each model is dealt with in a chapter (chaps. 2–6). Dulles, *Models of the Church*, 26–94.
61. Dulles, *Models of the Church*, 39.

trinitarian theology of church from a Reformed perspective, Robert Sherman converges the images into three rubrics to flesh out the purpose and call of the church: (1) the body of Christ, (2) the people of God, and (3) the temple of the Holy Spirit.[62] He is deliberate in selecting three to reflect the triunity of God—the Father, the Son, and the Holy Spirit.

From this brief glimpse into studies on biblical images of the church, we can glean a few important theological points about the church and identify its primary characteristics in God's mission. First, it is clear that the church occupies an irreplaceable position in God's mission of saving and blessing the world. Many of the images collated by Minear show that the calling of the church is theologically related to God's gift of salvation. The church is not a savior, but the church's calling is to testify about God and his work of saving the world through his people. Second, the variety of images for the church used in the Bible shows the theological heterogeneity and richness of the church. So rich and diverse are the images that it is impossible to draw out all their theological meanings or implications. However, we can identify key images and major descriptors of the church. Understanding both the church's true identity as one in God and its establishment in the world as connected to God's mission, we draw together what we consider to be key theological elements of the church in mission.

In dealing with the missionary calling of the church, the tendency has been to look into the call of the church to outreach. Here we are concerned with God's missional call of the church, and thus, the missionary dimension in the very establishment of the church. Robert Jenson, one of the most original and influential American theologians of the twentieth century, names what he considers to be the three dominant headings of ecumenical ecclesiology in the twentieth century: the people of God, the temple of the Spirit, and the body of Christ. These three clearly echo the Trinity. Jenson criticizes the unconnected treatment of the three ideas and their considerations as images and metaphors. He gives a systematic theological treatment

---

62. Robert Sherman, *Covenant, Community, and the Spirit: A Trinitarian Theology of Church* (Grand Rapids: Baker Academic, 2015).

"with epistemic seriousness by displaying the conceptual links" between the three.[63] He brings "people" and "temple" under "polity"[64] and connects that with the "body" ecumenically as "communion."[65] Our discussion in the previous section largely agrees with this. Jenson's emphasis on the connection between the three and the ecumenical influence is important.

Keeping our missiological interest in mind, I modify Jenson's list to include what I consider to be some of the Bible's chief characterizations of the church in God's mission: (1) the church as the covenant people of God, (2) the church as the body of Christ, and (3) the church as the Spirit-led servant-herald of God's kingdom. These three together highlight God's missionary calling of the church. The train of thought we will follow goes something like this: God calls the church as his people through the laying out of his covenant, and he lays the functional structure (inner and outer) in close relation to him, as a body is to the head. He exhorts the church's members by showing them how they may bodily function together through his redemption (the way of the cross as the expression of ultimate love) and charges them to carry out his call in and for the world. Our attempt is to describe the whole call in three parts using these three theological identities of the church.

The Covenant People of God

The church's primary identity and call is that it is God's people established and sustained in its covenantal relationship with him. If there is a mother tree or a progenitor among the images used to describe the church in the Bible, it should probably be the church as the people of God (e.g., 1 Pet. 2:9). This could even be considered the primary image of the church: the relationship between God and the church, or the church's claim of its relation with God. Claiming a special relationship with God can sound arrogant, and to understand oneself to be God's possession may sound chauvinistic and egoistic.

---

63. Jenson, *Systematic Theology*, 2:190.
64. Jenson, *Systematic Theology*, see chap. 25, "The Polity of God," 2:189–210.
65. Jenson, *Systematic Theology*, see chap. 26, "The Great Communion," 2:211–27.

Such claims could repel modern persons.[66] Yet, this is exactly what the church believes itself to be. In the history of ecclesiology, the idea of the church as the people of God came to special prominence when *Lumen Gentium* of Vatican II made it the central understanding of the Catholic Church in modern time.[67]

Although it is not very common to relate the church's identity as God's people with the theology of covenant, the theology of covenant establishes and explains the meaning of the church as the people of God. The very concept of the people of God comes from covenantal language: "For you are a people holy to the LORD your God; the LORD your God has chosen you out of all the peoples on earth to be his people, his treasured possession" (Deut. 7:6). The theological meaning of the people of God is found in the meaning and implications of the theology of covenant. The church's identity as the people of God is more than a metaphor; it is a description to which other metaphors gravitate[68]—the most significant, perhaps, being Israel or new Israel. Built on God's covenantal relationship with his people in the Old Testament, the church is imaged as the new covenanted people. Paul calls the church "the Israel of God" (Gal. 6:16), referring to either a distinct community (new Israel) or part of the older Israel. Other related metaphors include the chosen race, the holy nation, sons of Abraham, the remnant, and the elect.[69]

The church becomes the church in its covenant with God in Jesus Christ through the witness and power of the Holy Spirit. As mentioned, the name "people of God" is not a metaphor or a simile[70] as much as it is a description of the people's relationship with God. Because the church's identity as the people of God is built on Israel's covenantal relationship with God in the Old Testament, the meaning of the church's identity as God's people lies in the entire theology of the covenant—that is, old and new covenants. Old Testament critical scholarship has a long history of study of the covenant. As Ernest Nicholson summarizes, between Julius Wellhausen's pioneering work

---

66. Minear, *Images of the Church*, 68.
67. "*Lumen Gentium*," chap. 2.
68. "*Lumen Gentium*," 67–104.
69. Minear, *Images of the Church*, 71–104.
70. As rightly stated by Robert Jenson. See Jenson, *Systematic Theology*, 2:190.

in the late nineteenth century and the end of the twentieth century, scholarship has come full circle to affirm the distinctive and theologically rich covenant of God with Israel.[71] Serious considerations were given to the covenantal influences around Israel, such as the Hittite suzerainty treaties. While there are strong resemblances, the uniqueness of Israel's covenant, especially in connection with Israel's faith in God as the foundation of its identity, is undeniably clear. Nicholson concludes that the covenant did not form Israel into a cohesive tribe as such. What the Bible shows is "Israel's relationship with, and commitment to, Yahweh."[72] Furthermore, it is the idea of free choice that distinguishes the biblical concept of covenant: "The concept of a covenant between Yahweh and Israel is, in terms of 'cash value,' the concept that religion is based, not on a natural or ontological equivalence between the divine realm and the human, but on *choice*: God's choice of his people and their choice of him, that is, their free decision to be obedient and faithful to him."[73]

According to James D. G. Dunn, covenants, as they appear in the Old Testament, may be classified into four groups: (1) the covenant(s) with Abraham and the patriarchs, (2) the covenant with Israel through Moses, (3) special covenants (such as with David), and (4) the new covenant (Jer. 31:31–34).[74] More than any other New Testament writer, Paul makes the clearest distinction between the old and the new covenants. The author of Hebrews (in chaps. 7, 8, 9, 10, 12, and 13) also makes a clear separation, but not as sharp as Paul's, between the first and second (or "better") covenant. Luke's account of the Last Supper (Luke 22:14–23) follows Paul on the cup of "the new covenant" in Christ's blood (1 Cor. 11:25) as opposed to simply "blood of the covenant" in Matthew (26:27–28) and Mark (14:24). Both Paul and the author of Hebrews relate their theology of the new covenant to the promise of the new covenant as found in Jeremiah. In 2 Corinthians 3:4–18, Paul contrasts the old and the new, likening them to the letter

---

71. Ernest W. Nicholson, *God and His People: Covenant and Theology in the Old Testament* (Oxford: Oxford University Press, 1986).

72. Nicholson, *God and His People*, 191.

73. Nicholson, *God and His People*, 215–16 (emphasis original).

74. James D. G. Dunn, "Is the Old Covenant Renewed in the New? Chaplaincy Lecture 1998," in *Covenant Theology: Contemporary Approaches*, ed. Mark J. Cartledge and David Mills (Carlisle, UK: Paternoster, 2001), 35–40.

that kills versus the Spirit that gives life (v. 6). He then explicitly connects the old covenant to the Mosaic covenant and the new to faith in Jesus Christ. In Galatians 4:21–31, Paul allegorically differentiates God's covenants with Abraham and Moses and identifies the new covenant in Christ with Abraham's. Thus, Paul's new covenant is directly related to the covenant with Abraham, not the covenant with Israel through Moses.

The differentiation between the old and new covenants and their references is undeniable in Paul. The new is built on the covenant with Abraham and contrasted with the covenant with Israel through Moses. But what is their relationship? What does the old covenant have to do with the new? In his study of the biblical theology of covenant for contemporary understanding, Petrus Gräbe notes the interest in biblical theology of the covenant since the late twentieth century after a long lull. The new interest, he observes, centers on the relationship between old and new covenants, and between Jews and Christians and their self-understandings.[75] Does the arrival of the new supplant the old? Christian understanding has been ambiguous in history.

The new interest Gräbe references may in part result from a new perspective on the relationship between Judaism and Christianity that began with the influential works of E. P. Sanders in the 1970s.[76] While Christians and churches, especially Protestants, in the past have contrasted themselves with Jews and Judaism on the basis of their anti-Jewish understanding of Jesus and Paul, the attitude has changed among many Christians and even reversed for some, thanks to Sanders and others. This "new perspective" strongly and positively connects Judaism with Jesus and Paul.[77] James Dunn has reviewed the relationship between the old and the new covenants from this new perspective and sees more continuity than discontinuity from the old to the new. He says that the new covenant "is not a rejection of the old so much as a more effective implementation of the

75. Petrus J. Gräbe, *New Covenant, New Community: The Significance of Biblical and Patristic Covenant Theology for Contemporary Understanding* (Carlisle, UK: Paternoster, 2006), xviii.

76. Foremost in this is E. P. Sanders, *Paul and Palestinian Judaism* (Minneapolis: Fortress, 1977).

77. James D. G. Dunn, *The New Perspective on Paul* (Grand Rapids: Eerdmans, 2008).

old."[78] By recognizing the primacy of the covenant with Abraham, he concludes that "the old and new covenants should be seen not so much as two quite different covenants, but as two interpretations of the first covenant: the promise to Abraham."[79] While such a conclusion may not be fully persuasive—especially Dunn's argument for a single covenant and continuity between the covenant with Israel through Moses and the new covenant[80]—highlighting the continuity from Abraham to the new covenant is significant. The church in the New Testament understands itself as a fulfillment of the promise to Abraham and as sharing Abraham's blessing. Its identity is built on faith in God's fulfillment of his promise to Abraham. Thus, the covenant with Abraham and the new covenant are closely related, and the line of continuity between them cannot be ignored.

One common misconception about biblical covenant is that it is a contract or agreement. To clarify the matter, Joseph Ratzinger (later Pope Benedict XVI) suggests translating the Hebrew term *berith* (covenant) with "ordinance." He makes his case based on the Greek translation of *berith* with *diathēkē* and not *synthēkē* in the Septuagint. This, he says, shows that "the biblical content was not that of a *syn-theke*—a reciprocal agreement—but a *dia-theke*: it is not a case of two wills agreeing together but of *one* will establishing an ordinance."[81] If the English word "ordinance" contrasts with the other dimension we have just discussed—namely, freedom—it may be objectionable. But Ratzinger's point is well taken. The covenant belongs to God. It is his will that is engraved on it, and it is his gracious gift to humanity and all creation. "The 'covenant,'" declares Ratzinger, "is not a two-sided contract but a gift, a creative act of God's love."[82] As a free gift, it is given without compulsion.

78. Dunn, "Is the Old Covenant Renewed," 54.
79. Dunn, "Is the Old Covenant Renewed," 54.
80. In his response to the lecture, Mark Bonnington objects to Dunn's continuity thesis by saying, "But the old covenant of Torah in Moses is surpassed in the new covenant—[which is] more contrast than continuity." Mark Bonnington, "Is the Old Covenant Renewed in the New? A Response to James D. G. Dunn," in Cartledge and Mills, *Covenant Theology*, 66.
81. Joseph Cardinal Ratzinger, *Many Religions, One Covenant: Israel, the Church and the World*, trans. Graham Harrison (San Francisco: Ignatius, 1999), 48.
82. Ratzinger, *Many Religions, One Covenant*, 50.

Every community of people has its identity—cultural, ethnic, or national. As discussed elsewhere, God's identification or election of people does not strip human identities but supersedes and perhaps transforms them. The assimilation of cultures and traditions to God's call is part of a complex process that Christian communities pass through, most often subconsciously. God's calling of people, especially as a community, is never an easy process. The process of living out God's call is prone to misuse and miscarriage. From Christendom's domestication of God's call and politicking crusades to modern missionaries' attempts to "civilize" non-Western Indigenous peoples, Christian history shows the church's struggle to relate God's call and a people's sense of identity.

The Body of Christ

The image of the church as the body of Christ is distinctly Paul's, and we turn to his works for its purpose and meaning. While particular passages with the phrase in reference to the church appear quite clear, the diverse ways in which Paul uses images of the body as well as its members make it quite complicated. Minear observes that "the phrase 'the body of Christ' is not a single expression with an unchanging meaning" in Paul, as his "thought remains extremely flexible and elastic."[83] Not only does Paul use the term "body" in different ways for different purposes and meanings, but he even uses the phrase "body of Christ" for more than one meaning and purpose. In Romans 5–8, "the body of Christ" connects primarily to Christ's redemptive work through the crucifixion. For instance, in Romans 7:4, he writes, "You have died to the law through the body of Christ, so that you may belong to another." The use of "the body of Christ" for both salvific expression and the church's identity may have originated from the eucharistic and baptismal practices.[84] Paul expresses the meaning of eucharistic celebration by saying, "The bread that we break, is it not a sharing in the body of Christ?" (1 Cor. 10:16). A few passages later, he says, "We were all baptized into

---

83. Minear, *Images of the Church*, 173.
84. Arland J. Hultgren, "The Church as the Body of Christ: Engaging an Image in the New Testament," *Word and World* 22, no. 2 (Spring 2002): 125–26.

one body . . . and we were all made to drink of one Spirit" (1 Cor. 12:13).

The idea of the body of Christ does not usually appear in missiological discussions, probably because its meaning and intention relate to the church's inner dynamics and function. But as we will see, the image communicates a vital theology of the church in and for its mission, and some of its imagery reflects the world-directed aspect of the body.

Four of the letters in the New Testament bearing Paul's name (Romans, 1 Corinthians, Ephesians, and Colossians) employ the body-of-Christ imagery in connection with the church or community of believers. New Testament scholarship considers the first two as authentic letters of Paul and the latter two as disputed letters of Paul, so-called deutero-Pauline. There are marked differences in the discussions of the church as the body of Christ in Romans and 1 Corinthians (authentic letters of Paul) on the one hand, and Ephesians and Colossians (deutero-Pauline) on the other. While Romans 12:3–8 and 1 Corinthians 12:12–31 clearly refer to the churches in Rome and Corinth as the body of Christ, only in Ephesians and Colossians do we find the church explicitly described as the body of Christ (Eph. 1:22–23; 5:23; Col. 1:18, 24).[85] The difference is the use of "church" as a reference to a particular local congregation and to the universal church. Although there is no reason to think that the first two lack reference to the universality (or catholicity) of the church, they nonetheless refer to particular churches. The church's universality and its rootedness in each locality are equally important.

The Body of Christ: Diverse Gifts and Functions (1 Cor. 12:1–31; Rom. 12:3–8)

Whereas the Letter to the Romans is theological in nature and less specific in its situational reference, the first Letter to the Corinthians addresses local issues. Paul points to the Corinthians' questions several times (7:1; 8:1; 12:1), and the entire letter responds to issues they faced and questions they raised. The reference to the church as

85. Ian A. McFarland, "The Body of Christ: Rethinking a Classic Ecclesiological Model," *International Journal of Systematic Theology* 7, no. 3 (July 2005): 225.

the body of Christ in chapter 12 comes as a part of Paul's response to a question concerning spiritual gifts. It is a long section (chaps. 12–14) dealing with the proper functioning of the spiritual gifts. Paul's discussion of unity through diverse gifts and callings climaxes with the hymn of love (chap. 13). Paul is addressing a dispute arising out of competing ministries and assumed spiritual superiority, but he makes it clear that every ministry has its place and every gift is important because they are all gifts of the Spirit. Because there is only one Spirit, the many gifts—wisdom, knowledge, faith, healing, miracles, prophecy, discernment, tongues—are given freely by the same Spirit. Similarly, various acts of service are rendered to the Lord. The unity of the source (one Spirit, one Lord, and one God) is to be recognized for the variety of gifts, services, and activities.

As a way of relativizing the gifts and their corresponding services and activities, Paul then uses the metaphor of a body and its members. The basic point is that just as each part of the body contributes to the functioning of the whole body, each act of ministerial service achieves its goal and purpose in the working of the church. The success of one part is the success of all, the failure and suffering of one part is the failure and suffering of the entire body. Similarly, the church succeeds in unity as its members succeed and suffers if any part is suffering or failing. No member or form of ministry should consider itself superior and not in need of others, and no member should feel useless. Then Paul calls the church to support members and ministries that seem less honorable than others. The gifts are given by the Spirit, and the appointment of gifts is God's. Indeed, God has appointed apostles, then prophets, and then teachers. Each member's working for the common good, according to the specific appointments and gifts, is the point. For the functioning of each member, there is a better way—the way of love. This is the greatest gift that underlies every other gift (1 Cor. 13).

In Romans 12:3–8 Paul uses the same image as he deals with the functioning of the ministries in the church. Much briefer and appearing to be more general, this section of Paul's letter shows the unity of the church amid the diversity of members and their functions as in 1 Corinthians. Although some scholars suggest disunity prompted

Paul's words here, as in 1 Corinthians,[86] there are no indications
of such a problem. Instead, Paul exhorts Christians not to regard
themselves more highly than they should, but according to the faith
given by God. Paul's argument includes two important variations
from 1 Corinthians: (1) In 1 Corinthians 12:27, he says, "You are the
body of Christ and individually members of it," but in Romans 12:5,
he says, "We, who are many, are one body in Christ, and individually
we are members one of another." Although the difference may just be
linguistic, the added emphasis in Romans seems to be the interdepen-
dency of members of the church. (2) The list of functions in Romans
does not follow that of 1 Corinthians, and the functions appear more
general. Minear comments on this difference: "Proportionately more
attention was given [in Romans] to those gifts which by nature were
intended to be universally exercised by all the body's members."[87]

The similarities in these passages overwhelmingly outweigh the
differences. The church is the body of Christ, and the variety of its
ministries metaphorically parallels the body's variety of functions.
Despite its diverse ministries and spiritual gifts, the church is united
as the body of Christ, and its oneness lies in the one giver of all the
gifts, God's Spirit. In both places, Paul follows the discussion of the
variety of ministries and gifts with the way of love. In 1 Corinthians,
he tops the series of gifts with an encomium of love. And in Romans,
Paul similarly follows his discussion with a call for love, saying, "Let
love be genuine . . . ; love one another with mutual affection; outdo
one another in showing honor" (12:9–10).

The Head of the Body: Christ's Lordship and the Church (Colossians and Ephesians)

If Paul's emphasis in Romans and 1 Corinthians is on the church
as the body of Christ, Ephesians and Colossians stress Christ as the
head of the body. The high Christology in Colossians naturally places
the emphasis on Christ's lordship over the church. In fact, the first
clear phrase that Christ "is the head of the body, the church" (Col.

86. J. Paul Sampley, "The First Letter to the Corinthians: Introduction, Commentary, and Reflections," in *The New Interpreter's Bible*, ed. Leander E. Keck (Nashville:
Abingdon, 2002), 10:947.
87. Minear, *Images of the Church*, 195.

1:18a) comes as a part of the expression of the supremacy of Christ. Some suggest that Colossians 1:15–20 is a "citation of hymnic material in praise of Christ."[88] The first part, 1:15–17, deals with Christ's role in the creation of all, and the second part, 1:18–20, expresses his role in the redemption of all.[89] It almost seems surprising to read "the church" here, where Christ is shown to be the firstborn through whom all things were created and redeemed. The "head of the body" does not seem to image the human head and body connected by the neck. Rather, the head-body imagery seems to picture the total saving work of Christ, in which the church—clearly the universal, if not cosmic, church here—plays a role in the reconciliation of all things.

Not only is Christ the head of the church; he is "the head of every ruler and authority" (Col. 2:10). The entire text of the letter clarifies what it means to be the head—namely, to exercise authority and lordship over the body. By participating in his death (2:20) and being buried with him in baptism, Christians transition from being the body of flesh to the body of Christ (2:11–12).[90] By living in him and being freed from "philosophy and empty deceit, according to human tradition . . . and elemental spirits of the universe" (2:8), the church sustains its entity as the body of Christ.

We conclude our biblical survey of the church as the body of Christ with the Letter to the Ephesians, following Minear's treatment. For Minear, what we find in Ephesians about the body of Christ may be regarded as "the climax of the New Testament reflections on the body of Christ"[91] as the letter "provides an occasion for summarizing what has been said" about the topic.[92] The topic at hand is spread throughout this brief letter, beginning with God's exaltation of Christ by putting all things under him and making "him the head over all things for the church, which is his body, the fullness of him who fills all in all" (1:22–23). The God who exalted Christ saves us all by his grace in Christ Jesus. Christ became the peace between the once-alienated

88. Andrew T. Lincoln, "The Letter to the Colossians: Introduction, Commentary, and Reflections," in *The New Interpreter's Bible*, ed. Leander E. Keck (Nashville: Abingdon, 2000), 11:597.
89. Lincoln, "Letter to the Colossians," 11:597.
90. Minear, *Images of the Church*, 209.
91. Minear, *Images of the Church*, 213.
92. Minear, *Images of the Church*, 214.

communities, the Jews and the gentiles, who are united into one body through his redemption. Thus, even the gentiles, who once were far off, become "members of the household of God" (2:19).

As a part of the ethical exhortation, the author then lays out the eschatological unity of the body and shows the foundation of this unity in the first half of chapter 4. Through his death and resurrection, Christ descended into "the lower parts of the earth" and ascended "far above all the heavens" and "made captivity itself a captive" (4:8–10). In an interpretive style similar to the pesher of Qumran scrolls, the author of the letter gives Psalm 68:18 a soteriological interpretation stressing Christ's ascension.[93] The captivity he made captive refers "almost certainly" to "the principalities and powers, the rulers in heavenly places, including that 'last enemy' death,"[94] according to Minear. Standing on that victory of Christ, the letter exhorts that Christians should stand firm in the one body to which they have been incorporated, and they should live out the gifts assigned to them. The author spells out the very foundation of that unity of the body. When grouped into three as suggested by Charles Talbert, this "sevenfold basis"[95] of the unity of the church (Eph. 4:4–6) involves the sovereignty and oneness of God, as well as his unified work: "There is one body . . . one Spirit . . . [and] the one hope of your calling, one Lord, one faith, one baptism, one God and Father of all, who is above all and through all and in all" (Eph. 4:4–6).

It is the different gifts of this one and unified God that members receive. The list of gifts to equip the saints or members of the church in Ephesians is quite similar to the list of ministries in 1 Corinthians 12. Some would be apostles, some prophets, some evangelists, some pastors and teachers. The order of each list does not seem to matter much; what matters is the purpose of the gifts: equipping saints for building up the body of Christ, so it reaches maturity of faith in Christ, the head. The building up of the body happens as its members

---

93. Pheme Perkins, "The Letter to the Ephesians: Introduction, Commentary, and Reflections," in *The New Interpreter's Bible*, ed. Leander E. Keck (Nashville: Abingdon, 2000), 11:420–21.

94. Minear, *Images of the Church*, 216.

95. Charles H. Talbert, *Ephesians and Colossians*, Paideia Commentaries on the New Testament (Grand Rapids: Baker Academic, 2007), 109.

grow into Christ, the head of the body, through whom the body functions properly.

In this brief discussion, we have seen that "the body of Christ" is a biblical portrayal of the church's functional structure in relation to God. Our discussion has shown that the key concept is the church's relationship with God. This relationship has been established in and through the redemptive work of God in Christ, and the image of the redemption in his body thus carries the image of what the church should be. Vatican II's *Lumen Gentium* powerfully expresses this point by saying, "Christ, having been lifted up . . . has established His Body which is the Church as the universal sacrament of salvation."[96] The eucharistic image is always present in the shadow of the body of Christ, and the call to love is insistent in each text we have examined. The image of the church as the body of Christ is most meaningful in the context of the church's worship. The church originated as Christ's body, and its sustenance depends on its faithful growth into that body. Thus, vital connection with God in Christ through the power of the Spirit is the very foundation of the church as an entity. The church is the church only in its bond with Christ. This imagery of the church is also about functional unity. The church is endowed with different gifts and called to diverse ministries. Significant in this function is the missionality or apostolicity of the church.

The imagery of the church as Christ's body is used in different ways. In Romans, it is used to exhort Christians not to think highly of themselves but according to the measure of faith and gifts given by God. In 1 Corinthians, it reminds God's people of their unity amid their different calls. Colossians and Ephesians stress the work of God in Christ and urge members to grow into him, the head of the body. If the image of the body is the focus in Romans and Corinthians, the image of the head dominates in Colossians and Ephesians.

Spirit-Led Servant-Herald of God's Kingdom

We have discussed both the church's identity as the people of God, with its foundation in the theology of the covenant, and the church's functional image as the body of Christ, seen in specific writings in the

---

96. "*Lumen Gentium*," chap. 7, par. 48.

New Testament. We now look into the church's call to be a servant and a herald of God's good news of the kingdom. This call cannot be drawn from specific books or passages but has to be drawn from the overall message of the New Testament. While some texts appear stronger or more specific than others on the call to serve and to proclaim (to be the channel), any attempt to nail them down to specific texts often misses other aspects because of the richness of the message and how the point is spread across texts. In historical hindsight, this seems to have been the case with the so-called Great Commission texts and evangelistic missionary works in the modern missionary movement. While the missionary call is no less than being sent to proclaim the gospel (Mark 16:15), to witness (Luke 24:48; Acts 1:8), and to disciple the nations (Matt. 28:16–20), the focus on such particular texts left out other aspects of the call.

Among studies discussed earlier, we have noted Stanley Skreslet's work, which connects the church's identity to the service of God's good news. The good news, according to the teaching of Jesus, is about the coming of the kingdom of God (Mark 1:15). The kingdom is at the center of his ministry and message during his Galilean ministry. As New Testament scholars, including N. T. Wright and Joel Green, have explained, in the Bible's concept of the kingdom, the coming of the King, or God becoming king of the whole world, is the main point.[97] Moltmann's comment about the Greek term *basileia* (kingdom) is helpful; he says it "can mean both the actual rule of God in the world, and the universal goal of that divine rule."[98] Time and history are important in the understanding and identification of God's kingdom message and work. The kingdom of God is an eschatological promise. At the heart of the Christian faith is that the King (the Messiah) has come, the King is coming, and the King will come again. The kingdom message, the message of his coming, has to do with the eschaton, or end time, which was inaugurated at the coming of Jesus Christ in human history, in the incarnation-ministry-death-resurrection-ascension event of Christ. The New Testament

97. N. T. Wright, *Surprised by Hope: Rethinking Heaven, the Resurrection, and the Mission of the Church* (New York: HarperOne, 2008), 202; Joel Green, *Kingdom of God: Its Meaning and Mandate* (Bristol, UK: Bristol Books, 1989).
98. Moltmann, *Church in the Power of the Spirit*, 190.

is replete with the promise of Christ's return (parousia), in which the full measure of the kingdom is promised. In the interim period between his first coming and his final coming, the church has been given the opportunity to serve the kingdom. We live in the present, empowered by the anticipation of the fulfillment. To quote Moltmann again, "Through his mission and his resurrection, Jesus has brought the kingdom of God into history. As the eschatological future the kingdom has become the power that determines the present. The future has already begun. We can already live in the light of the 'new era' in the circumstances of the 'old' one."[99]

This opportunity for the human community to taste the kingdom and anticipate the final kingdom is both a blessing and a call for the church. The church is tasked to serve the kingdom, to bear witness to the goodness of God's kingdom to the entire creation. Skreslet's good-news-centered study of the mission of the church and his focus on the examples of the disciples in the New Testament are important directives here. He identifies five missional models of the disciples that combine the proclamation of the good news itself and its demonstration in actions through "a *commitment to live* in ways that publicly affirm the transforming power of God's love."[100] These five images that make up much of the book are (1) announcing good news, (2) sharing Christ with friends, (3) interpreting the gospel, (4) shepherding, and (5) building and planting.[101] Beyond the works surrounding the gospel of Jesus Christ (announcing, sharing, and interpreting) are caring (shepherding) for the needy and the work of planting and building up communities of faith as God's temple (1 Cor. 3). The church is called to care for, to build up, and to serve human beings and creation within and without, as much as it is called to learn, to preach, to live with, and to diffuse the gospel message.

During the past few centuries, efforts to share the gospel of Jesus Christ have been popularly discussed under the rubric of "evangelism" in Protestant circles and under "evangelization" among Catholics. These terms derive from the Greek noun *euangelion* ("gospel" or

---

99. Moltmann, *Church in the Power of the Spirit*, 192.
100. Skreslet, *Picturing Christian Witness*, 27 (emphasis original).
101. Skreslet, *Picturing Christian Witness*, 29–32.

"good news") and its verb, *euangelizein*, which most English Bibles translate as "preach" or "proclaim the gospel." Polarizing debates among Protestants about how the gospel is best served in evangelism have cast a shadow over the term itself; it is ironic that the "good news" has been eclipsed by its conceptual debates. In a paper read during the Methodist Conference of 1992 in Newcastle-upon-Tyne, Kenneth Cracknell made a historical reflection on the English terms "evangelism" and "evangelization," noting that "rare indeed are the sightings of either term before the mid-nineteenth century."[102] Even the English evangelical revival leaders John and Charles Wesley never used them. It was the Second Great Awakening in North America that introduced the word "evangelism" into common parlance, such that it became synonymous with "revivalism."[103] Because the tradition that popularized the word often used it to criticize those it considered not centered on the good news, the term and the concept acquired an oppositional stance and were associated with a tendency to polarize.

The Corinthians' struggle regarding different spiritual gifts for ministries may have to do with the varying priorities and values they assigned to respective gifts and ministries. Protestant history has shown various forms of such contentions. Early twentieth-century history of Protestant ecumenical cooperation was composed of two movements: the Faith and Order movement, which centered its attention on doctrinal questions, and the Life and Work movement, which focused on social services. Although many leaders were involved in both, the two tended to compete with each other. While Faith and Order seemed to understand itself as dealing with the core Christian issue, Life and Work responded in the early 1930s with its slogan, "Doctrine divides and service unites." The two movements came together in the late 1930s to form the WCC.[104] Such a tension between

102. Kenneth Cracknell, "Protestant Evangelism or Catholic Evangelization? A Study in Methodist Approaches," (paper presentation, Methodist Sacramental Fellowship Public Meeting, Methodist Conference, Newcastle-upon-Tyne, 1992), 1. https://www.sacramental.org.uk/uploads/5/0/0/9/50096105/protestant_evangelism _or_catholic_evangelization.pdf.

103. Cracknell, "Protestant Evangelism or Catholic Evangelization?," 3.

104. See Willem Adolph Visser 't Hooft, *The Genesis and Formation of the World Council of Churches* (Geneva: World Council of Churches, 1987).

word (proclamation, doctrine) and deed was revived again in the 1960s between evangelicals and ecumenicals.

The ecumenical-evangelical dissension that roiled the Protestant world between the 1960s and the early twenty-first century took similar paths but with much more intensity. The priorities of evangelism, or proclamation, and socially inclined service were set against each other as antithetical ways of serving the gospel. Much has been done to rescue the beautiful English word "evangelism" from its polarized use. Like the ecumenists of the early 1930s, evangelicals from the majority world introduced a holistic understanding of evangelism that integrates proclamation and socially oriented service.[105] For such a purpose, a definition of Christian missions first voiced in the World Mission and Evangelism Conference of 1963 has become popular; it says that Christian mission "must be the common witness of the whole church bringing the whole gospel to the whole world."[106]

On the meaning of evangelism, Thomas Thangaraj suggests a return to the English origin of the word, calling it "goodnewsing." It is about preaching or proclamation of the good news of Jesus Christ. But it need not be limited to preaching. The evangelistic call is "living the good news" and "being the good news," he insists.[107] Understanding evangelism as the announcement or proclamation of the gospel, N. T. Wright asserts the importance of the New Testament perspective, saying that "the gospel in the New Testament is the good news that God (the world's creator) is at last becoming king and that Jesus, whom this God raised from the dead, is the world's true lord."[108] Jesus himself and the gift of new and everlasting life in him are what we call the gospel or the good news. They are the center of Christian identity. The universality of the gospel (as good news for all) obligates the church to share it with the entire creation. The

105. See Brian Woolnough and Wonsuk Ma, eds., *Holistic Mission: God's Plan for God's People*, Regnum Edinburgh 2010 Series (Oxford: Regnum Books International, 2010). For a history of holistic mission, see the chapters by Al Tizon, Samuel Jayakumar, and Tito Paredes.

106. Ronald K. Orchard, ed., *Witness in Six Continents: Records of the Meeting of the Commission on World Mission and Evangelism of the World Council of Churches Held in Mexico City December 8th to 19th, 1963* (London: Edinburgh, 1964), 175.

107. M. Thomas Thangaraj, *The Common Task: A Theology of the Christian Mission* (Nashville: Abingdon, 1999), 79.

108. Wright, *Surprised by Hope*, 226–27.

very raison d'être of the church is in its call to serve this good news in its life, work, and words.

Jesus is not only the good news himself, but he is also the model servant-herald of the good news. We conclude this section with Paul's plea for a servant's mind centered on Christ crucified. In Philippians 2:6–8, Paul presents one of the most powerful statements about Jesus's incarnation in a solemn and rhythmic style that scholars often call a hymn:[109]

> who, though he was in the form of God,
>   did not regard equality with God
>   as something to be exploited,
> but emptied himself,
>   taking the form of a slave,
>   being born in human likeness.
> And being found in human form,
>   he humbled himself
>   and became obedient to the point of death—
>   even death on a cross.

As much as it has been referred to as "the Kenosis [self-emptying] hymn," this may also be called a hymn of the incarnation. In his incarnation, Jesus voluntarily took the most humiliating form by emptying himself to take on not only human form but the lowest form of humanity. His self-humbling act reaches to the point of death, the death on the cross. Because Christ did this, God has highly exalted him (v. 9). This hymn of the self-emptying Christ is introduced by Paul (in v. 5) with the words "Let the same mind be in you that was in Christ Jesus." For Paul, the crucified Christ is both the content of the preaching (1 Cor. 1:23) and the mindset demanded of Christians. As Asian theologian Kosuke Koyama insists, "the crucified mind" is what makes a missionary a missionary.[110] The good news is costly and its blessing rich.

109. Morna D. Hooker, "The Letter to the Philippians: Introduction, Commentary, and Reflections," in *The New Interpreter's Bible*, ed. Leander E. Keck (Nashville: Abingdon, 2000), 11:501.

110. Kosuke Koyama, "What Makes a Missionary: Toward a Crucified Mind, Not a Crusading Mind," in *Mission Trends 1: Crucial Issues in Mission Today*, ed. Thomas F. Stransky and Gerald H. Anderson (New York: Paulist Press, 1974), 117–32.

5

FULLY GOD AND FULLY HUMAN

Theology and Culture in the Mission of God

Culture and Theology

As the world was becoming relatively internationalized in the late nineteenth and early twentieth centuries, new ways of viewing human cultures through modern sociology and cultural anthropology were surfacing. Greater interactions between people groups and deeper attempts to understand the nature of human societies and cultures produced interest in, as well as recognition of, the need for serious consideration of cultures in theological studies. Kathryn Tanner aptly says that through "a long and circuitous route," we have seen a transition in the meaning of culture from a notion of high culture or civilization to "the anthropological notion of culture."[1] Although this transition happened in the English-speaking world, the route included the influence of the German concept of *Kultur*.[2] In this new anthropological sense, culture came to refer to different

---

1. Kathryn Tanner, *Theories of Culture: A New Agenda for Theology*, Guides to Theological Inquiry (Minneapolis: Fortress, 1997), 3.
2. Tanner, *Theories of Culture*, 9–12.

ways of living in groups, "the customs of particular peoples viewed as distinct self-contained wholes."[3] The transition to this new notion of culture seems to have taken quite a long time in the West. Writing in the early 1980s, American anthropological missiologist Paul Hiebert said that the two uses of the word "culture" were still mixed.[4] Anthropologists came to use the word "culture" in a new way. They began to relate a single culture to other cultures, and the idea of cultural plurality became central. According to this modern anthropological understanding, culture is universal, human centered (as opposed to nature centered), and bound in social groups. It is about the entire way of life that a social group has subconsciously developed. Thus, there are as many cultures as there are social groups. Because of this, modern anthropology came to view cultural diversity in a relativistic and nonjudgmental way. While human communities make cultures, culture also makes or forms people through its norms.[5] As a social being, the human being is essentially cultural. To be human is to be cultural.

The late-modern or postmodern way of thinking has been increasingly critical of the modern anthropological understanding of culture, even as the concept adapts to a postmodern mentality. The modern certainty of knowledge, including the anthropological idea of culture's integral wholeness, has been called into question by postmodern critics. Scholars who relate modern anthropological work on culture with postmodern challenges may express their views differently,[6] but most agree that postmodern criticism[7] does not sup-

3. Tanner, *Theories of Culture*, 19.
4. Paul G. Hiebert, *Anthropological Insights for Missionaries* (Grand Rapids: Baker Academic, 1985), 30.
5. Tanner, *Theories of Cultures*, 25–29.
6. Here, we may compare the expressions of Michael Rynkiewich and Kathryn Tanner. Rynkiewich exclaims that "anthropology changed in the 1980s and 1990s, but missiology did not get the news[!]" See Michael Rynkiewich, *Soul, Self, and Society: A Postmodern Anthropology for Mission in a Postcolonial World* (Eugene, OR: Cascade Books, 2011), 8. Kathryn Tanner outlines the various challenges and criticisms by postmodern thinkers but observes a rather minimal or limited change. She concludes that "very few of the aspects of that [modern] understanding have actually been discarded. Most are retained with more or less their modern senses." See Tanner, *Theories of Culture*, 56.
7. See, e.g., Tanner, *Theories of Culture*, 38–56.

plant modern understanding; rather, it reshapes or reconstructs it.[8] What seems to have happened is that postmodern criticism created an alternative version of the modern understanding of culture. Without making a clear-cut boundary, a postmodern-influenced understanding now coexists with the modern conception of culture, and most anthropologists operate in between. Overall, the postmodern criticism strengthens the modern understanding as it helps to adapt the concept of culture to historical processes.

Dramatic changes in world history during the twentieth century necessitated conceptual adaptations of culture to historical developments and realities. Even if the basic conception of culture remains the same, the mode of its application has expanded. If those who defined culture in the early twentieth century drew from human situations and experience in regional and conceptually unified settings, global movements of people, technological developments, and multiplying information in the late twentieth and early twenty-first centuries have drastically altered human experience and behavior. Closer proximity between human groups produced deeper self-reflection and mutual respect. At the same time, more encounters and interactions between people of different cultures produced competing notions of culture. Robert Schreiter helpfully identifies at least two main groups of concepts in his study on how cultural concepts relate to theological thought. The first he calls "integrated concepts of culture," which "depict culture as patterned systems in which the various elements are coordinated in such a fashion as to create a unified whole."[9] The other arises out of critiques by postcolonial and globalization thinkers and takes seriously social changes and the struggles for social power. He calls this second group of concepts "globalized concepts of culture," since "they reflect the tensions and pressures arising out of the globalization process."[10] For postmodern-postcolonial thinkers, "culture is something to be constructed rather than discovered, and

8. Tanner summarizes the result of postmodern work under "reconstruction," (Tanner, *Theories of Culture*, 56). Although Rynkiewich is emphatic in his expression of the change, his book largely follows the modern notion of culture mixed with some postmodern views.

9. Robert J. Schreiter, *The New Catholicity: Theology between the Global and the Local* (Maryknoll, NY: Orbis Books, 1997), 47–48.

10. Schreiter, *New Catholicity*, 53–54.

it is constructed on the stage of struggle amid the asymmetries of power."[11] These two understandings reflect the complexity of culture today. As much as the two ideas function together, they also reflect the reality of multiple cultural belongings. Individuals today often have layers of cultural identities in which they function.

Coming back to culture-theology relations, whether culture follows theology or theology follows culture is hard to determine precisely. Theology's proposition of God as the way to fathom the mystery of life is bound to lead a culture on a particular faith path. However, everything we can make sense of in life, including our beliefs, employs and is influenced by our cultures too. Thus, our cultural presuppositions also direct the trajectory of our faith. Here, theologians not only take different positions but differ in their understanding of culture's place with respect to theology.[12] To some, theology is a part of culture;[13] to others, culture is within theology;[14] still others see them as separate entities and reflect on how they may be theologically and socially related.[15] Following our earlier discussions of God's incarnation (chap. 1) and the covenant theology of the people of God (chap. 4), where the "otherness" of God featured prominently, we differentiate theology and culture and see God's mission as relating the two. T. F. Torrance's differentiation between God's relation to the world as "infinite differential" and the world's relation to God as "a created necessity," mentioned in chapter 1, guides our thought here. Aside from his existentialist orientation, Paul Tillich's correla-

11. Schreiter, *New Catholicity*, 54.

12. D. Stephen Long, *Theology and Culture: A Guide to the Discussion* (Eugene, OR: Cascade Books, 2008), 53.

13. The most well-known classic advocate is Ernst Troeltsch. In Tanner's attempt to draw theological methodology using anthropological contributions, she takes this position, following the arguments of various theologians, including Gordon Kaufman and David Tracy. See Tanner, *Theories of Culture*, 61–92.

14. This, as shown by Long, is the position of George Lindbeck. See Long, *Theology and Culture*, 53.

15. Based on his classic study of *Christ and Culture*, in which he outlines the relation under five types, roughly between "Christ of culture" and "Christ against culture," Richard Niebuhr has been placed on the "Christ against culture" side of the spectrum (Tanner, *Theories of Culture*, 62). Some place him there because he does not offer any criticism of the "Christ the transformer of culture" position (see Long, *Theology and Culture*, 63–65). If not directly "against" culture, Niebuhr could be seen as looking for the "conversion of culture" to God.

tion of theology and culture makes good sense: "Religion as ultimate concern," he writes, "is the meaning-giving substance of culture, and culture is the totality of forms in which the basic concern of religion expresses itself."[16]

The Christian faith we are dealing with in this volume and the effort we have outlined to make sense of Christian thought with respect to the theology of mission are products of our time and our way of thinking, which in turn is bound and dominated by the spatial and temporal knowledge we have acquired in our time period. Every interpreter should admit that we pick and choose texts, ignoring things we consider irrelevant or hard to understand. Our contexts—in terms of space, time, and the worldviews they produce—form us into who, what, and how we are, and we operate accordingly. Thus, we can only understand the gospel in and through our culture. Yet to regard God and one's faith in God as solely "within culture," as a product of one's culture, is to misunderstand the faith which is placed "beyond" oneself (and thus, one's culture). The "beyond" or "within" debate will always remain an argument; neither can ever be proven or disproven. But the very fact that our faith perceives God and God's business beyond our culture should not be downplayed. In theological studies, we study our faith with the conviction that the object of our faith is a reality beyond our ability to prove or disprove. In other words, the line of thought we assume in the present study is that the God in our faith is not only more than us but also beyond us.

Nicaean-Chalcedonian Theological Anthropology

Today, there are many Christian studies on culture. They range from considering the practical use of culture for effective ministerial and missionary tools to analyzing the cultural captivity of theological hermeneutics in the postmodern and postcolonial world. In this chapter we draw a few conclusions about what the gospel in its theological aspect has to do with the plurality of human cultures. We are not relating cultural studies to theological studies as such but are looking

16. Paul Tillich, *Theology of Culture*, ed. Robert C. Kimball (Oxford: Oxford University Press, 1959), 42.

into a theological foundation for understanding human cultures in God's mission. What have culture and cultures to do with God's mission, what potential role can human cultures play, and what essential threat can they pose? As indicated in chapter 1, we locate such a foundation within God's mission to the world, which is ultimately represented in his incarnation. The incarnation, as discussed in Torrance's work, is central in the relationship between God and the world, and consequently in the relationship between theology and culture. Torrance goes so far as to claim that in the Christian faith the incarnation, the decisive action of God in Christ, is the only possible way to God in space and time.[17] Human culture is central in human existence in space and time. The doctrine of incarnation has many potential implications for understanding God's relation to humanity, and culture is a key component in that relation.

The Nicene Creed (AD 325) describes the humanity of Jesus Christ as the Son of God who came down from heaven for us and our salvation and was incarnate by the Holy Spirit. Although the creed emphasizes the divinity of Christ, somewhat overshadowing its statement on Christ's humanity, its declaration on the incarnation of Christ for the salvation of the world clearly shows his humanity. As discussed in chapter 1, God's entry into human history—that is, into time and space—in the person of Jesus Christ is simply extraordinary. This is the expression of God's love: his identification with his creation to the extent of limiting himself to his created time and space. To what extent did Christ become human in his incarnation (that is, taking on human flesh)? Was he partially human and fully divine, as many in the pew today may understand him to be? It is easy to think of him as fully divine and deceptively or partially human. The Council of Chalcedon (AD 451) provided a clear answer more than one hundred years after the Council of Nicaea, explicating the manner by which that expression of God's love had come to pass.

The Council of Chalcedon, perhaps the best-documented ancient church council,[18] is known for leading to the schism of the church

17. Thomas F. Torrance, *Space, Time and Incarnation* (Oxford: Oxford University Press, 1969), 75.
18. "The Acts of the Council of Chalcedon," one of the longest surviving texts from the ancient world, provides the details of the council, making the council

that created the group now called the Oriental Orthodox Church. The main and intended outcome of the council was the rejection of the Christologies of Nestorius and Eutyches, and by extension, alleged Monophysitism (Christ has one single divine nature) and Miaphysitism (both divine and human in Christ are united in one nature). The council's work, which became known as the Chalcedonian Definition, became a defining authority of orthodoxy in the West. Eastern Christianity, however, struggled with it for a long time and ultimately permanently divided over it. Even Byzantine Christianity in the East, which affirmed the definition with the West, took a long time to settle on it.[19] Politics played a significant role both immediately and at a later time. Who the Monophysites and Miaphysites were became difficult to determine. Whether the Miaphysite position of Cyril of Alexandria was condemned is a matter of debate because he was referenced positively and warmly by the council.[20] The Miaphysite position was later adopted as a non-Chalcedonian (or even anti-Chalcedonian) position in the East, such as in Armenia.[21]

The most significant portion of the Chalcedonian Definition is in the final section:

> Following the holy fathers, we all with one voice confess our Lord Jesus Christ to be one and the same Son, *perfect in divinity and humanity, truly God and truly human, consisting of a rational soul and a body, being of one substance with the Father in relation to his divinity, and being of one substance with us in relation to his humanity, and is like us in all things apart from sin* (Hebrews 4:15). He was begotten of the Father before time in relation to his divinity, and in these recent days, was born from the Virgin Mary, the *Theotokos*, for us and for our salvation. *In relation to the humanity, he is one and the same Christ, the Son, the Lord, the only-begotten, who is to be acknowledged in*

"possibly the best-documented event in Roman, or early church, history" (see the preface to Richard Price and Michael Gaddis, eds. and trans., *The Acts of the Council of Chalcedon*, 3 vols. [Liverpool: Liverpool University Press, 2005], ix). Thanks to Price and Gaddis, the texts are now available in English.

19. Richard Price, "The Development of Chalcedonian Identity in Byzantium (451–553)," *Church History and Religious Culture* 89, nos. 1–3 (2009): 307–25.

20. Price and Gaddis, *Acts of the Council of Chalcedon*, 1:62–68.

21. See, e.g., Theo Maarten van Lint, "The Formation of Armenian Identity in the First Millennium," *Church History and Religious Culture* 89, nos. 1–3 (2009): 251–78.

two natures, without confusion, without change, without division, and without separation. The distinction of natures is in no way abolished on account of this union, but rather the characteristic property of each nature is preserved, and *concurring into one Person and one subsistence, not as if Christ were parted or divided into two persons, but remains one and the same Son and only-begotten God, Word, Lord, Jesus Christ*; even as the Prophets from the beginning spoke concerning him, and our Lord Jesus Christ instructed us, and the Creed of the Fathers was handed down to us.[22]

As a further explication of the Nicene Creed, this statement clearly attempts to explain the humanity of Christ and how it is to be affirmed with his divinity. In the process, it affirms two natures in one person, a sticking point for non-Chalcedonians, some of whom regarded the definition as Nestorian, even though the clear mention of the *Theotokos* (a reference to the Virgin Mary as "the mother of God") was intended against Nestorius's teaching. The passage quoted above clearly lays the emphasis on the humanity of Christ without subverting the divinity. The second half of the passage is devoted to expressing the humanity and explaining how the humanity is to be affirmed together with the divinity.

As we have mentioned before, the theological significance of the doctrine of incarnation for relating gospel and culture is significant. Chalcedon's statement on Christ's humanity offers a firm foundation to relate Christ and culture even more explicitly than the more generalized Nicene statement. The affirmation of Christ to be "truly human . . . being one substance with us" states his full identification with humanity. Not only has he entered our story, but he has become one among us; he is us. As a full human being, he entered one culture and was limited to that culture. The Synoptic Gospels' presentations of Jesus's life and ministry leave no doubt that he belonged to the Jewish culture of his time, while he was also truly the only begotten Son of God. The Gospels' story of Jesus's life is fully set in the Jewish culture but is punctuated throughout by signs of his oneness

22. Quoted in Alister E. McGrath, ed., *The Christian Theology Reader*, 3rd ed. (Oxford: Blackwell, 2007), 281–82 (emphasis mine). For a more literal and less inclusive translation, see Price and Gaddis, *Acts of the Council of Chalcedon*, 1:59.

with God. This dual belonging, in all its mystery, is what the ancient creeds attempt to state explicitly.

No group in the christological debate denied the divinity of Christ, but did any of the so-called non-Chalcedonians oppose his humanity? In a reexamination of the Chalcedonian tradition from a non-Chalcedonian viewpoint, Indian Syrian Orthodox theologian-historian V. C. Samuel points out how Western historians have wrongly painted the non-Chalcedonians and how terms like Monophysitism (the notion of a single divine nature in the person of the incarnate Christ) do not represent the group accused of it.[23] With respect to the non-Chalcedonians' view on the humanity of Christ, Samuel concludes that no theologian or church leader of the tradition "has at any time criticized the council [of Chalcedon] for its affirmation of the fullness and reality of Christ's humanity."[24] What then did they oppose in the council? The primary opposition was against the language of "two natures," which they considered the Nestorian heresy condemned by the Council of Ephesus in 431.

Chalcedon's explication of the humanity of Christ should not be taken as an emphasis on it. The point is Christ's fullness in his divinity and humanity. The Son of God is the Son of Man. From the human cultural viewpoint, Christ is both beyond culture and fully in culture. In him, we see God's affirmation and transcendence of culture. Without sacrificing his transcendence of human culture, we can affirm his immanence within humanity and its diverse cultures.

Biblical Hermeneutics of Mission and Human Cultures

Whether a religion is missionary or not depends on the universality or particularity of its core message. If its basic teaching is addressed to, and has a promise only for, an exclusive group or community or society, such a religion is not missionary. It does not concern others and has no message for them. For a religion to be missionary, it must

---

23. Opposing the term "Monophysitism," Samuel uses "non-Chalcedonian." V. C. Samuel, *The Council of Chalcedon Re-examined*, Indian Theological Library (Delhi: ISPCK, 1977), xxi.

24. Samuel, *Council of Chalcedon*, 200.

have a promise for all, have a message for all, and be addressed to all. The most basic question about the missionary nature of Christianity or the church is about the universality of its message. Is the Christian message of salvation addressed to all? Is Christ the savior of all? If so, that message has to be passed on to everyone. The call is for those who have heard it to pass it on to others. In other words, the apostolicity of the church (or the sending of the church) is built on its catholicity (or universality), to use the four marks of the church we discussed in the previous chapter. Is the core message of Christianity—namely, the gospel of Jesus Christ—meant for all? Does the Bible address its message to all people and does its core message have a promise for everyone? The same question applies to the gospel's relation to the diverse cultures. Does the Bible, apparently written within the Jewish culture, have relevance for and is it applicable to non-Jewish cultures? Our interest lies with this intercultural question (between Jewish and non-Jewish cultures), but it is dependent on the missionary question.

It may be surprising to see these questions raised in the last chapter of this study. In the previous chapters, we have traversed major dogmatic themes of Christianity for missiological meanings and foundations. Our discussions have led to this set of most basic missiological questions: Did Jesus understand himself as being sent to save all people? Why should we think that his teachings and ministries, which were carried out exclusively among Jews in Palestine, are applicable to others? Is it true, as some scholars contend, that the universal message of Christianity is Paul's invention? Our focus is on cultural implications, but we begin by briefly outlining the reasons for biblical theology's universal application as a missiological foundation.

Most Christians today in the post-Western missionary era tend to assume that Jesus is the savior of all and that the Bible's message is universally valid. The modern missionary movement has left an indelible universal mark on most ordinary Christians. But a closer reading of the Bible leaves no doubt that it is the story of one particular people, the Jews, and that Jesus's ministry was almost exclusively limited geographically and culturally to Jewish people. For some, Christianity as a universal religion is Paul's invention and not Jesus's.[25] Paul undoubtedly saw himself as an apostle set apart for gentiles: "But when [God], who had set me apart even from my mother's womb and called me through His grace, was pleased to reveal His Son in me so that I might preach Him among the Gentiles, I did not immediately consult with flesh and blood," he declares (Gal. 1:15–16 NASB). The historical-theological rationale for gentile missions is laid out by Paul in his Letter to the Romans (15:8–21). Some debate whether Paul encouraged others to follow him in gentile missions,[26] but Paul's defense of the universal claim of God's salvation is unquestioned. As Luke's account in Acts shows, gentile missions was a natural outcome of the church's expansion, and Paul was not alone in the ministry to gentiles. However, the facts that Paul has to make a strong defense of it (Rom. 15) and that a meeting of the leaders in Jerusalem (Acts 15) had to decide on it beg the question.

What scholars call "the scandal of particularity," undeniably present in Judaism and Christianity, is a natural obstruction to the universality of both traditions' teachings and thus their missionary character. In Judaism, God's election of the nation of Israel among many nations, the singling out of this tiny community among many communities, seems to defy the universality of his love and care for all. This is the religion of Jesus and the pattern he followed. At times, he seems to have followed it quite closely: "I was sent only to the lost sheep of the house of Israel" (Matt. 15:24). Furthermore, limiting God's salvation through one man from Nazareth who lived and died some two thousand years ago is scandalous at best to non-Christians.[27] Typically, the act of electing one excludes the rest, and thus election is a theological problem of missions. While the Bible is the story of this small people called Israel and this man called Jesus, a careful reading of the entire book shows that the God of the Bible deeply cares for others (the nonelect). Scholars investigating this puzzling issue see a

25. Gerd Lüdemann, *Paul: The Founder of Christianity* (Amherst, NY: Prometheus Books, 2002).

26. On this debate, see Robert L. Plummer, *Paul's Understanding of the Church's Mission: Did the Apostle Paul Expect the Early Christian Communities to Evangelize?* (Waynesboro, GA: Paternoster, 2006).

27. Lesslie Newbigin, *The Open Secret: An Introduction to the Theology of Mission*, rev. ed. (Grand Rapids: Eerdmans, 1995), 66.

deep tension between particularity and universality throughout the
Bible. In the words of Old Testament theologian Walter Brueggemann, "It is important in doing Old Testament theology to keep in
purview the tension between YHWH as *the God of Israel* ('I shall be
your God') and YHWH as *God of all peoples*."[28] This is important
because "in all the fundamental texts," Brueggemann observes, "the
tension between the *God of Israel* and the *God of nations* is apparent everywhere."[29]

The tension between the particular (Israel) and the universal (all
nations) is not static but dynamic, showing active movement between
them. In the movement from the particular to the universal, missiologists came to identify an important pattern in God's missionary
motif. While most missiologists of the past focused on a universal
dimension in the Bible as the foundation for missions, theologians of
missions came to use the dynamic tension and movements between
particularity and universality as a missiological foundation. The
important work of Johannes Blauw in the early 1960s, for instance,
is an argument based almost solely on the universalism in the Old
and New Testaments.[30] Others identify the significant role of the
particulars in the universal. As mentioned, Lesslie Newbigin draws
out biblical patterns of election as a movement from particular to
universal:

> God, according to the biblical picture, although he is the creator, ruler,
> sustainer, and judge of all peoples, does not accomplish his purpose
> of blessing for all peoples by means of a revealer simultaneously and
> equally available to all. He chooses one to be the bearer of his blessing
> for the many. Abraham is chosen to be the pioneer of faith and so to
> receive the blessing through which all nations will be blessed. Moses
> is chosen to be the agent of Israel's redemption. . . . The church is a
> body chosen "to declare the wonderful deeds" (I Pet. 2:9).
>
> This is the pattern throughout the Bible. The key to the relation
> between the universal and the particular is God's way of election. The

---

28. Walter Brueggemann, *Old Testament Theology: An Introduction* (Nashville:
Abingdon, 2008), 247.

29. Brueggemann, *Old Testament Theology*, 248 (emphasis original).

30. Johannes Blauw, *The Missionary Nature of the Church: A Survey of the
Biblical Theology of Mission* (New York: McGraw-Hill, 1962).

one (or the few) is chosen for the sake of the many; the particular is chosen for the sake of the universal.[31]

The one for the sake of many, the particular as a way to the universal, has become a hermeneutical key in reading the Bible in connection with God's mission. By the beginning of the twenty-first century, theologians made excellent hermeneutical refinements, together with substantive biblical engagements, for the theology of mission. The works of Christopher Wright with strong emphasis on the Old Testament[32] and Michael Goheen on the New Testament[33] are splendid examples. They show God's mission by tracing the entire biblical story. Critical in this connection is the new interest in Jewish restoration as the framework to interpret the Gospels' narrative about Jesus, which we will see later. By locating mission as the fulfillment of the eschatological expectation of God's restoration of his people on Mount Zion, these scholars make a strong biblical argument for mission. They demonstrate the significant point that the Bible is a testimony of God on mission through the individuals and the people he calls, prepares, and equips. It is the story of God creating, redeeming, and transforming the world through his servant-heralds, as he has called them to be.

Quite similar to Newbigin's observation is Richard Bauckham's "hermeneutic for the Kingdom of God." Critically responding to the words of Rabbi Jonathan Sacks, the Chief Rabbi of Britain, that "God is universal, religion is particular," Bauckham states his foundational point about God's mission in the Bible by saying "*God* is both universal and particular."[34] Like Newbigin, he sees the movement from the particular to the universal, or from the one to the many, as a "prominent aspect of the narrative shape of the [entire]

31. Newbigin, *Open Secret*, 68. Newbigin continues to discuss this pattern in a number of other publications. See, e.g., "The Logic of Election," in *The Gospel in a Pluralist Society* (Grand Rapids: Eerdmans, 1989), 80–88.

32. Christopher J. H. Wright, *The Mission of God: Unlocking the Bible's Grand Narrative* (Downers Grove, IL: IVP Academic, 2006).

33. Michael W. Goheen, *A Light to the Nations: The Missional Church and the Biblical Story* (Grand Rapids: Baker Academic, 2011).

34. Richard Bauckham, *Bible and Mission: Christian Witness in a Postmodern World* (Grand Rapids: Baker Academic, 2003), 9 (emphasis original).

biblical story."[35] He locates the key to understanding God's kingdom theme and the church's universal mission in that movement. The mission of the church is to serve God's kingdom, which he defines as "the achievement of God's purposes for good in the whole of God's creation."[36] What Bauckham sees in a biblical pattern of the movement from the particular to the universal is what Wright and Goheen apply in detail in their books and what Newbigin discusses under the doctrine of election. What distinguishes Bauckham and makes us follow him here is his hermeneutical emphasis together with his brevity and precision.

He shows the movement of biblical narrative from "the one to the many" through "four different strands in the biblical metanarrative."[37] These strands are (1) from Abraham to all families of the earth, (2) from Israel to all the nations, (3) from the king who rules from Zion to the ends of the earth, and (4) to all by way of the least.[38] Of these four, the first three are thematic trajectories of the narrative. The trajectory from Abraham to all the families of the earth is "the trajectory of blessing."[39] The second theme, from Israel to all the nations, is "the trajectory of God's revelation of himself to the world," and the third trajectory "that moves from God's enthronement of David in Zion is the trajectory of rule, of God's kingdom coming in all creation."[40] Not only do the three represent three different themes (blessing, revelation, and rule), they also represent the singling out of a person (Abraham), a nation (Israel), and a place (Zion).[41]

The fourth strand, "to all by way of the least," is clearly distinguishable from the first three. Whereas the first three are based on Old Testament narratives with their New Testament interpretations and implications, the fourth strand is drawn wholly from the New Testament and is based on Paul's interpretation of the way of the cross in the Christ event. Using 1 Corinthians 1:26b–29, Bauckham shows how "God singled out the poor and the powerless, choosing to begin

35. Bauckham, *Bible and Mission*, 12.
36. Bauckham, *Bible and Mission*, 11.
37. Bauckham, *Bible and Mission*, 27.
38. Bauckham, *Bible and Mission*, 28–54.
39. Bauckham, *Bible and Mission*, 27.
40. Bauckham, *Bible and Mission*, 27.
41. Bauckham, *Bible and Mission*, 41.

his work with them, not because God's love does not extend to the social and cultural elite, but actually for the sake of the wealthy and the powerful as well as for the poor and the humble."[42] Paul is intentional in this regard, Bauckham notices. The way to the strong has to be through the weak "because the strong can receive the love of God only by abandoning their pretensions to status above others."[43] The weak must choose to help the strong abandon their arrogance and their dependence on status in order to receive God's love and grace. Thus, the weak and their weakness become salvific for the strong and the rich. Jesus's identification with and love for the marginalized as presented in the Gospels show the same theme. Bauckham argues that, for Paul, this is God's way as also paradigmatically shown in the cross: "The claim that God is to be encountered and salvation found in a crucified man—a man stripped of all status and honour, dehumanized, the lowest of low—is the offence of the cross."[44]

Thus, the biblical pattern of movement from the one to the many, from the particular to the universal, pivots in the idea of the least for the sake of all. What does this pattern, the movement from one to many, from the few to all, and from the least to everyone, tell us about the gospel-culture relation we have been pursuing? First of all, this is the way by which God reaches all. This is God's way of mission and God's missionary principle. Second, it is also God's way of dealing with human cultures. God entered a particular culture for the sake of all the cultures; he did not deal with human cultures in a general and universalized way. The incarnation is not just a general rule but a specific event in human history and culture. Such a particularized means has important universal implications. As mentioned, the pattern of choosing one or few does not exclude the larger human society. The one chosen is for the sake of all others.

The gospel-culture question seen in the light of this particular-universal tension affects how one understands the relationship between Christianity and Judaism. Jesus's Jewishness and his treatment of his Jewish culture are at the heart of the issue. How did Jesus identify with his Jewish culture, and how did he relate to his culture with

42. Bauckham, *Bible and Mission*, 50.
43. Bauckham, *Bible and Mission*, 50.
44. Bauckham, *Bible and Mission*, 52.

his kingdom message? Biblical and theological studies have a long history of interesting positions and interpretations on the matter. The different theories fall on a spectrum between what theologians call supersessionism and a position that sees Jesus's mission to be the restoration of Judaism. Historic Christian supersessionists believe "that the church has taken the place of the Jews as the elect people of God"[45] and that because of their rejection of Jesus the Messiah of God, God has disfavored the Jews, the descendants of Abraham according to the flesh.[46] Such a position would have had strong support in the Christian world up to the middle of the twentieth century, or more specifically until the horrendous Holocaust and its worldwide condemnation. As global political courses changed and the relations between Christians and Jews became more favorable, we also saw changes in biblical interpretations by both Jews[47] and Christians. In addition to "the new perspective" on Paul is the "third quest for the historical Jesus,"[48] which locates his mission within Jewish restoration eschatology. The two most prominent and original contributions on this thesis come from E. P. Sanders and N. T. Wright. Sanders explicitly deals with the topic as a central driving force of Jesus's ministry in Judaism,[49] while Wright uses it to frame the entire gospel narrative in the first-century Jewish expectation of restoration.[50]

On the basis of Christ's fully divine and fully human personhood—but with the risk of overgeneralization—it is safe to say that Jesus operated fully within his culture while his mission transcended that culture even as it sought to transform it. In other words, the substance of his teaching and ministry was not contained in or limited to his culture, though he functioned fully within it. I believe such an understanding is within the thesis of the restoration of Israel. The restorative message of Jesus looks countercultural in its immediate

45. Bruce D. Marshall, "Christ and the Cultures: The Jewish People and Christian Theology," in *The Cambridge Companion to Christian Doctrine*, ed. Colin E. Gunton (Cambridge: Cambridge University Press, 1997), 82.

46. Marshall, "Christ and the Cultures," 83.

47. See, e.g., Matthew Hoffman, *From Rebel to Rabbi: Reclaiming Jesus and the Making of Modern Jewish Culture* (Stanford, CA: Stanford University Press, 2007).

48. N. T. Wright, *Jesus and the Victory of God*, Christian Origins and the Question of God 2 (Minneapolis: Fortress, 1996), 83–124.

49. E. P. Sanders, *Jesus and Judaism* (Philadelphia: Fortress, 1985), 61–119, 335–40.

50. Wright, *Jesus and the Victory of God*, see esp. 150–97.

context while fully operating in the larger cultural framework. His counteractions and provocative judgments against Pharisaic hypocrisy, for example, defied aspects of cultural practices but served the larger goal of the society and its cultural values. Scholars who emphasize the transformational aspects within the restoration teaching of Jesus have good points. Steven Bryan argues that Jesus's restoration mission was combined with his announcement of the national judgment, which he suggests altered "the central elements of Jewish restorationism."[51] The foundation of Jewish identity is its covenantal call, in which it was failing. By issuing the message of repentance and announcing the coming power of God in his kingdom, Jesus challenged the society to be renewed in God's power. N. T. Wright's brief summary of Jesus's kingdom message in the first-century context of Judaism is most enlightening on this point:

> Jesus was affirming the basic beliefs and aspirations of the kingdom: Israel's god is lord of the world, and, if Israel is still languishing in misery, he must act to defeat her enemies and vindicate her. Jesus was not doing away with that basic Jewish paradigm. He was reaffirming it most strongly. . . . He was, however, redefining the Israel that was to be vindicated, and hence was also redrawing Israel's picture of her true enemies. This, after all, has good historical parallels; it was the basic move made in some way or other by every Jewish sect, including the followers of John, and the Essenes, and the various factions during the war of 66–70. Jesus, then, was offering the long-awaited renewal and restoration, but on new terms and with new goals. He was telling the story of Israel, giving it a drastic new twist, and inviting his hearers to make it their own, to heed his warnings and follow his invitation.[52]

Every culture has good and bad elements. In the case of Judaism, the core of its cultural identity is its being called or elected to serve God. The message of the coming of God's kingdom and the actions of King Jesus demanded both change and renewal. As scholars like John Riches conclude, Jesus attacks the beliefs and works of Phariseeism, Essenism, and Zealotism—whose exclusivism and

51. Steven M. Bryan, *Jesus and Israel's Tradition of Judgement and Restoration* (Cambridge: Cambridge University Press, 2002), 236, 243.
52. Wright, *Jesus and the Victory of God*, 173.

anti-Hellenism did not represent the goal of God's election and call of Israel—through his teaching of repentance and the good news of the kingdom, while holding to the agenda of Israel's restoration.[53] The impending kingdom of God rests instead on forgiveness and repentance, love and inclusion.

Implications of the Pattern and the Hermeneutic

The example of Jesus's kingdom teaching in a particular Jewish history and culture has universal significance for how one ought to see the gospel-culture relation. Jesus modeled both affirmation and transformation of culture. If we are to draw a theology of culture, this is a key principle. The biblical hermeneutical principle has shown us how the God of the Bible acts. He chooses one to show what the rest should do. He chooses one to bless all, calls the few to reach the world. Yes, Jesus was incarnated not only in history in general but in a particular space and time, the specific culture of first-century Judaism. The particularity reveals God's depth of care and love for the people and the urgency of transformation. It models God's dealing with the world he loves.

Like a seed planted, the gospel takes root and grows in each culture. Yet the goal of planting that seed is not to produce one tree in isolation; it is to produce as many trees as the cultural variety allows. Each culture has as much potential to grow God's love as to resist his grace. God does not love the world only corporately; God loves each person, each people group, each nation, and calls each to renewal within their own ways. To reach the "horizontal world," consisting of different people, traditions, and cultures, the biblical principle is one for many, or the few for all. To reach the "vertical world" of high- and low-status people, powerful and weak, the biblical principle is the way of the cross, the final path taken in his incarnate form in the world. Not only does he reach different people in their ways of life, he reaches the marginalized and the least of them by becoming one of them.

---

53. John Riches, *Jesus and the Transformation of Judaism* (New York: Seabury, 1982), 168.

We may close this discussion with another paradoxical reality about the gospel-culture question implied in the tension between the particular and the universal, or figuratively in this case, the vertical and the horizontal. We acknowledge something special about being chosen or called, such as Abraham and Israel were, but when taken as a model of the calling of each and every person (as in every member of the church, Rom. 12), the pattern of the call shows the uniqueness of each call. The particularity of the gospel's relation to the Jewish culture of Jesus modeled the particularity of the gospel's relation to each culture. The gift of freedom that comes with God's grace, as taught by Paul, is that every person can approach the gospel from their own situation. As he fervently argued in his Letter to the Galatians, Paul taught that the gentile Christian did not need to approach the gospel through the Jewish tradition. The gospel can be at home with each culture directly, without the interference of another culture or tradition. This process of inculturation (or in-culturation) will take a particular and perhaps unique path for each culture. Thus the manner by which the gospel relates with and transforms a culture may be unique for each culture.

Inculturation, as missiologists have come to realize, is not the end or the final stage in the process. It is a part of the larger process in which "interculturation" is a natural companion element. No one receives the gospel directly and exclusively from God in heaven! The gospel is passed from one to the other horizontally, starting with the one who is the gospel himself, the Son of God and Man, who is fully God and fully human. God's gift of salvation in his grace, therefore, is passed from one human being to another, from one cultural group to another. In his unique rhetorical style, Paul asks, "But how are they to call on one in whom they have not believed? And how are they to believe in one of whom they have never heard? And how are they to hear without someone to proclaim him? And how are they to proclaim him unless they are sent?" (Rom. 10:14–15a). Then, echoing Nahum 1:15, Paul exclaims, "How beautiful are the feet of those who bring good news!" (Rom. 10:15b). Proclamation is an essential part of the process of passing on God's good news. Not only did Jesus perform miracles; he taught and proclaimed the good news of the kingdom. From person to person, from culture to culture, this good news of God's kingdom is to be shared.

The history of Christianity in its global context shows how it often comes to identify with the culture of the people. On the one hand, if it is embraced by just a fraction of the people and seen as a minority religion, Christianity tends to operate on the fringes as a foreigner's religion. Missionaries often look for ways to relate the religion with the people's culture to make it their own. Christians and missionaries often burden themselves with indigenizing the religion to the culture of the people. On the other hand, people groups that embrace Christianity quickly often face cultural crisis first. Once the new faith settles into the people's way of life (culture), it becomes theirs. When Christianity becomes their own and closely related to their culture, they then face the danger of making the religion their own too exclusively. Christianity is a shared religion. Each people group can own it in such a way that all culture groups can own it for themselves. Thus, it is to be possessed so that it fully influences the community while it is also to be shared so that others may have it as their own.

CONCLUSION

A Summary of a Theology of Mission

We are at a crossroads in the history of Christianity, where traditional Western Christianity meets the new majority world (or non-Western world) Christianity. Theological understanding and interpretations tend to become multifarious along confessional, cultural, and regional lines. The rise of contextual theology, or the recognition of the contextual nature of every theology, helps to define the multi-faceted nature of theology. Furthermore, with the proliferation of theological disciplines, theology has become complex. Nevertheless, the constants of theology do not really change. At the heart of every Christian theological endeavor are the reflections on God, humanity, the world, and the hope for salvation. In the context of the twentieth- and twenty-first-century renewal of trinitarian theology and the accompanying ecclesiological revival, we have reread theology by giving special attention to that aspect we call theology of mission. As a result, we define theology of mission and try to identify its location in the disciplinary gamut of theology.

Christian understanding of God is distinguished by the place and role of Jesus Christ in the oneness of God. The belief in Jesus as the incarnation of God recalibrates the very concept of God in that Jesus the Son of God is one with God the Father, even as he operates distinctly from God the Father. When taken together with God as experienced—that is, God the Spirit—what we have is the triune God. We began our inquiry into the theology of mission with this doctrine of the Trinity. We argued that theology of mission is rooted in this Christian theological core of the Trinity. In doing this, we took our theological cue from Thomas Aquinas's use of "missions" of the Second and Third Persons of the Trinity. The triunity of God is complex and its explanations in the globalizing and pluralistic world are multiplying. New interpretations from Asian Brahmanic (Hindu) and Taoist backgrounds have enriched the understanding immensely.

In the history of trinitarian study, theologians have explained the nature of God by distinguishing God *in esse* (in his being or immanence) from God in his works of revelation (economy). This distinction widened in the course of history, resulting in the separation and sequencing of the one God and the triune God, as Karl Rahner has alleged. While Rahner's controversial axiom (that economic Trinity is the immanent Trinity and the immanent Trinity is the economic Trinity) suggests a permanent erasure of the distinction, we do not agree that the distinction should be erased. The twentieth-century interest in the Trinity centered the discussion of the relationship between the immanent Trinity and the economic Trinity. Rahner's critique of the separation between the two serves as a significant factor for the rising interest. In the light of the ensuing debate, we concluded that while it is theologically implausible to separate the two, it is helpful to maintain the distinction between immanent Trinity and economic Trinity. Karl Barth's insistence on the interwovenness of the two is helpful if their distinctions are also maintained.

Theology of mission, we argued, deals with God's works in the world and thus relates primarily to the economic Trinity. The distinct-yet-inseparable relation of the immanent and economic Trinity resonates with the relationship between the discipline of theology and theology of mission as its subdiscipline. While the larger discipline of theology concerns itself with inquiring into God's being, nature, and work, theology of mission tends to focus on God's work in the world. Embedded in the economic Trinity, theology of mission deals with God's relationship with the world and tackles his redemptive mission of his creation. It probes God's salvific works and his call of the people to participate in his mission to redeem and transform the entire creation. More specifically, it inquires into God's redemptive work as witnessed to and carried out by his people in the frontier between faith in both him and his work in Christ on the one hand, and the absence of such faith on the other.

Broadly defined, salvation consists in God's work of restoring life in the world. In the divine economy, this work of God bestowing salvation came through the Son. As testified in classic works such as Athanasius's *On the Incarnation* and Anselm's *Cur Deus Homo?* (*Why God Became Man*), the doctrines of the incarnation and salvation are conjoined in Christian theological thought. The incarnation of the Son is the means for God's mission of saving his creation. In and through the kenotic act of becoming human, his self-sacrificing death, and his resurrection, Jesus Christ redeems the world, justifies the rebellious humans, and restores their relationship with God. The Christian Scripture is endowed with a variety of images of this salvific work and how it impacts humanity.

From a variety of biblical images and motifs, Christians have been theorizing about how God works out the salvation of the world. We dealt with this topic in chapter 2 and the first half of chapter 3. From the three classic theories of the Western church, we demonstrated that the theories have multiplied. We attempted to profile them in the global church context, taking the current demographic changes of Christianity into serious consideration. We assembled the theories into four groups based on their dominant emphases and motifs. While regional, confessional, and cultural factors play important roles, the ecumenical atmosphere of the period has also somewhat globalized all the salvific themes. We named the first of the four groups of theories "God's Triumphal Deliverance from Oppressions and Sufferings" and argued that this group of theories is dominant in the majority world today under themes such as liberation, Christ the Victor, and healing. Even if some of these are either sidelined or waning in the West, they represent the dominant salvific thoughts in the majority world. The much more juridical group we rather awkwardly named "God's Redemptive Forgiveness" includes such traditional Western theories as penal substitution, justification, and ransoming sacrifice.

Although Western in origin and nature, they spread globally among Protestants and Catholics and have been adapted as leading themes of soteriology.

The third group of theories was compiled together based on understanding salvation as union with God. The first theory, *theosis*, was identified quite exclusively with Orthodox churches but has now started to influence other Christian communities. In the contentious global atmosphere, the theme of reconciliation has received new life. Reconciliation, together with shalom, has also received new interpretation in connection with ecology and care for the creation. In this group, we included a lesser known yet significant interpretation of salvation from the Hindu Brahmanic worldview, calling it "oneness with God." The inclusion showcases the dynamic of salvation and its adaptability to new worldviews for wider and deeper meaning. The last group of theories surrounded the understanding of salvation as the life-giving work of God. The topic of new birth has played a significant role in traditional Protestant evangelicalism. Salvation as life-giving has its meaning in the emerging theology of creation and creation care. Restoration of life cannot just be about human life; it is about the restoration of the entire creation.

The scope of salvation especially in connection with other (non-Christian) religions is a topic of great interest in the religiously pluralistic context of the globalizing world. We closed our study of salvation with this topic in the second half of chapter 3. Two seemingly contrasting biblical points served as the bases of the debating positions—namely, that God wants everyone to be saved (1 Tim. 2:4; 2 Pet. 3:9) on the one hand, and that there is salvation only in Jesus Christ (John 14:6; Acts 4:12) on the other hand. Whether we discuss the three well-known Christian attitudes to other religions (exclusivism, inclusivism, pluralism), the four views of salvation (evidentialists, post-Enlightenment, inclusivists, pluralists), or the three soteriological positions (restrictivism, inclusivism, and universalism), it all comes down to where one stands between the two poles of God's desire to save all and salvation only in Christ. A wise conclusion was made by the World Mission and Evangelism Conference (of the WCC) in 1989: "We cannot point to any other way of salvation than Jesus Christ; at the same time, we cannot set limits to the saving power of God."[1]

Along with interest in the theology of mission comes a revival of ecclesiology. Dormant for centuries, ecclesiology received the greatest attention with an ecumenical spirit in the twentieth century. Quite significantly, a core theological question has been the mission and raison d'être of the church. From different confessional and theological viewpoints, the worldwide Christian community came to recognize the missionary calling of the church as a reason of its being. The Bible uses a wealth of images and metaphors to illustrate the church as a spiritual entity. The images highlight different aspects of the church—its goals, meanings, and reasons for being. From our discussion of the biblical images of the church, we concluded that the church has an irreplaceable role in the mission of God. Our review of the images and their discussions in relation to the church's role in God's mission led us to three chief metaphors: the church as a covenant people of God (its identity in God), the church as the body of Christ (its functional structure), and the church as Spirit-led servant-herald of God's kingdom (its task). The three are closely related and are conceptually linked. God's call is first and foremost to a covenantal relationship, which recognizes his absolute authority. The body imagery illustrates the diverse means to function in unity. The church's missionary task is rooted in its identity as a servant and a herald of God's kingdom.

In making a case for the foundation of Christian mission as God's missional work in the world, we considered the question of human culture and society to be exceptionally important. Defining culture as having everything to do with life in human societies, we see faith, and thus theology, "within" and "beyond" culture. Here we disagree with theologians who limit theology within human culture as much as we differ from those who separate theology from culture. We find a foundation to deal with the theology-culture relation in the historic faith statement of the Nicene Creed, especially as redefined in the Council of Chalcedon. The Chalcedonian Definition presents Christ as "truly God and truly human." Its expression of the incarnate Jesus

---

1. Fredrick R. Wilson, ed., *The San Antonio Report: Your Will be Done; Mission in Christ's Way* (Geneva: World Council of Churches, 1990), 32.

to be "truly human . . . being one substance with us" signifies the totality of Jesus's identification with humanity and its cultures. Even the opponents of the Council of Chalcedon agreed on this statement of Christ's humanity. Yet as "truly God" Christ is distinguished in every sense from human beings. Theology of human culture, we argued, is best defined between Christ's "truly God and truly human" identity and works.

We concluded our discussion on a Christian theology of God's mission in the world in the last chapter by addressing the question of whether biblical Christianity (or the Bible of the Christians) is missional at all. Whether a religion is missional or not depends on its universal claim and appeal. Is the God of Israel also the God of all people? Does God in Christ intend to engage and save only the elect or all people of the world? The "scandal of particularity" embedded in the theology of election is a natural obstruction, yet it is also a clear way of God's mission in the Bible. Following the lead of some biblical interpreters, we traced the passage from particularity to universality, a pattern defined by the principle of choosing (or calling) a few for the sake of all. We considered this to be the biblical pattern. The tension between particularity and universality defines the biblical way of God's missionary engagement in the world. It is this same tension that clarifies the gospel-culture relation in that God reaches all when Christ's incarnation reaches each particular culture by embracing and transforming it.

INDEX